Palmistry Guide

(An Easy way to learn Palmistry)

Nisha Ghai
(Director, Institute of Palmistry, New Delhi)

Books For All
Delhi-110052

Distributed by
D.K. Publishers Distributors (P) Ltd.
4834/24, Ansari Road, Darya Ganj,
New Delhi-110002
Phones: 23278584, 23278368, 23261465,
e-mail: dkpd@del3.vsnl.net.in
visit us at: www.dkpd.com

First Published 2003

ISBN 81-7386-254-0

Published by
Books For All
(an imprint of Low Price Publications)
A-6, Nimri Commercial Centre,
Near Ashok Vihar Phase-IV,
Delhi-110052
Phones: 27401672, 27452453
e-mail: lpp@nde.vsnl.net.in
visit us at: www.lppindia.com

Printed at
D K Fine Art Press P Ltd.
Delhi-110052

PRINTED IN INDIA

Introduction

The lines on the palm show the graph of our unconscious mind. Just as a good cardiologist can study and interpret the graph of heart (E.C.G.) in a same way, a good palmist can interpret the significance of the lines on the hand.

When a person who is ignorant of the science of palmistry finds a palmist telling him about his past, present and future, he might get an impression that a miracle is unfolding before his eyes. But what the palmist is doing, in fact, is only reading the unconscious mind of his client.

Nisha Ghai

W - 21, Greater Kailash - 1
New Delhi - 110048

Contents

Chapter - 1

The Scope of Palmistry

Why does a man go to a palmist ? One only goes to a palmist to know about his love, carrier or what vocation should he choose. He wants to know the answer of his personal problems. By predicting the future a good palmist can not only help one in taking the right decisions but can also suggest remedies to over come his problems.

Palmistry as a Carrier

Every common man wants to know about his future and to some extent also tries to make it favourable. By studying shape of hand and lines an experienced palmist can advise best for future prospects and by doing so he can also help one in choosing a good profession for himself / herself.

Palmistry for Popularity

A good palmist is always surrounded by inquisitive people. They are keen to show him their hand in order to know about their future. A good palmist has good net work of relations and friends.

Chapter – 2

History of Palmistry

The science of palmistry was a well developed science in ancient India. It was a part of the science known *SAMUDRIKA SHASTRA*. The practitioners of this science studied the shape of the various organs of the body and indicated the tendencies and traits of that person while forcasting his future.

A small part of *SAMUDRIKA SHASTRA* was called *HAST SAMUDRIKA*. From India this science spread to China, Tibet, Rome, Greece, Iran and other countries.

The famous Greek Philosopher, Aristotle was an erudite scholar of palmistry. They were Gypsies who spread the knowledge of this science in European Countries. Most of the scientific investigations on palmistry were done in the nineteenth and twentieth centuries in Western Countries.

Now Institute of Palmistry in New Delhi, India, is conducting new research in the field of scientific palmistry and has found it to be related to human psychology. While writing this book I have kept in view both western palmistry and *Samudrika Shastra* of Indian palmistry but in the end conclusion is based on my own experience, study and research.

Chapter – 3

Palmistry a Science

Palmistry is a science. Just as new experiments are being conducted every day in various sciences with old laws getting discarded and the new one discovered, palmistry is also undergoing the same process.

How Scientific Palmistry Is ?

Hand is a mirror of our personality. Its size, shape, texture, skin pattern, finger prints, length of fingers and Mounts of our hand reveal our basic instincts and make us aware of our own personality potentials and talents. All these features along with lines make our future. After knowing and understanding these features we can know hidden capacity of the person.

Lines of our hand are not the creases on hand but they represent the activity of our unconscious mind (Hindus call it *MANN*).

More lines in our hand means more active mind. According to the research of Prof. Dayanand (Head of the Institute of Palmistry) the Mounts on our hand work as magnetic centers which attract electric currents of brain and lines on the palm show the path of those currents. Reading the lines is the reading the hidden capacity of a person.

Prof. Dayanand also says that 25% of somatosensory area of the brain is related to both the hands which indicates the close relation between brain and hand.

Palmistry is study of unconscious mind. The desires which lie dormat in our unconscious build the blocks of future. These longings show themselves as lines of palm. When we read lines of palm we, in fact, read the unconscious because only this reading of unconscious that leads one's capability to read the future.

Lines are subject to change

From my experience, I have noticed that the lines of palm are subject to change. Our will power, optimistic /passimistic thinking and positive or negative behaviour may be the course of this change.

The job of a good palmist is not to just predict future of a person, but is also to encourage him/her to fight against obstacles and to help one in building confidence for changing his lines in the desired way.

Chapter – 4

Which Hand is to be examined: Right or Left?

This is a very common question : Which hand of a client should be studied – right or left ?

According to the ancient Indian Palmistry (*HAST SAMUDRIKA*) a woman's left hand and a man's right hand should be preferred for study.

According to Western Palmistry both the hands of the person should be studied, left hand upto adolescent age and after that priority should be given to right hand or active hand. The hand with which we write.

Our conclusion on this point is that the importance should be given to both the hands since the non active hand reflects our unconscious mind which we have brought with us in the forms of genes and the active hand reflects our conscious mind which we have changed through our efforts.

The signs of both the hands should be considered. The signs which are similar in both the hands can lead to certain definite conclusion. But where the signs are not similar the deciding factor should be signs of active hand. (The one with which a person writes.)

Moreover, there is no need to distinguish between men and women and young or matured person in this regard.

Chapter – 5

Chirognomy or Chiromancy

Palmistry has two branches :

1. Chirognomy
2. Chiromancy

<u>*Chirognomy*</u> It is the knowledge of shape of hand, Mounts, texture, quality of hand, length, width and thickness of hand and fingers.

It reveals about the basic nature and temperament of the person.

<u>*Chiromancy*</u> It is the knowledge of lines which reveals about the ups and downs in the person's life and about his or her past and future.

Chapter – 6

Chirognomy: Shape of Hand

Let us take Chirognomy first. French palmist D. Arpentingny has divided hand into seven categories. This categorisation has been widely accepted.

<u>*Elementary hand*</u> - See Fig. 1- a

The palm of elementary hand is small, thick and hard and the thumb is short. People having this category of hand generally have under developed brain. They have a tendency of getting exited and voilent very quickly.

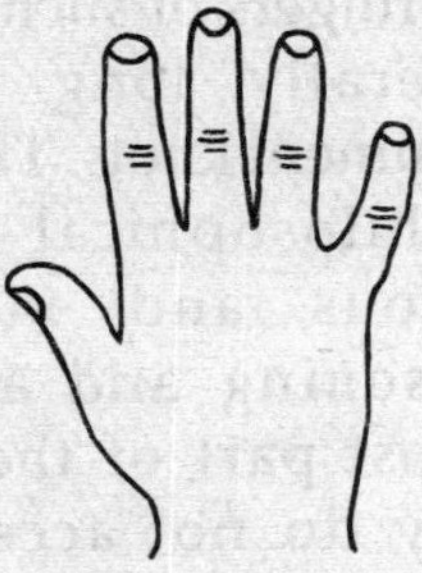

Fig. 1-a: Elementary Hand

<u>*Square Hand*</u> - See fig. 1 - b

Square hand has square palm, with even the finger tips having also square shape. People with such hands are active, have more physical strength, practical thinking and with less imagination. They are organised. They respect religion, law and order rather obediently.

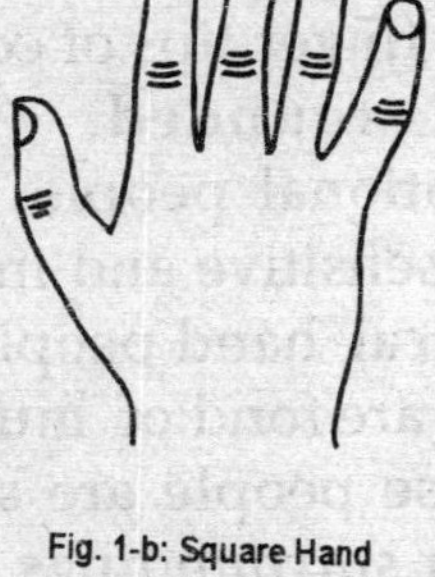

Fig. 1-b: Square Hand

<u>Spatulate Hand</u> - See fig. 1 - c

The third category is the spatulate Hand. Finger tips of such a hand are like a spatula and heavy. People with these hands have zest for work but have less stamina. They get excited soon.

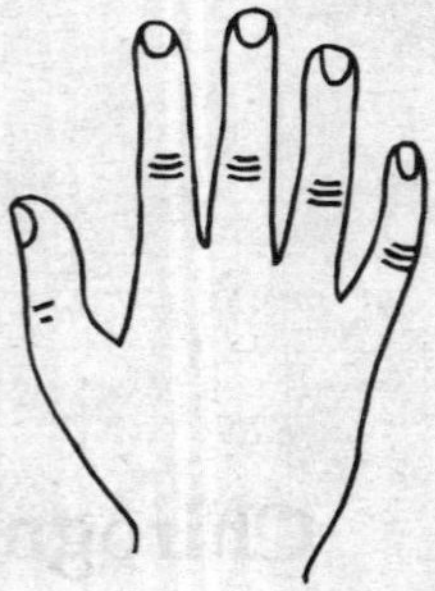

Fig. 1-c: Spatulate Hand

<u>Philosophic Hand</u> - See fig. 1 - d

The fingers of such a hand are generally long and have prominent knots. The owner of a philosophical hand are curious and methodical. Reasoning and analysis is almost part of their nature. They do not accept things without analysing them. They have more mental power than physical. They are good thinkers.

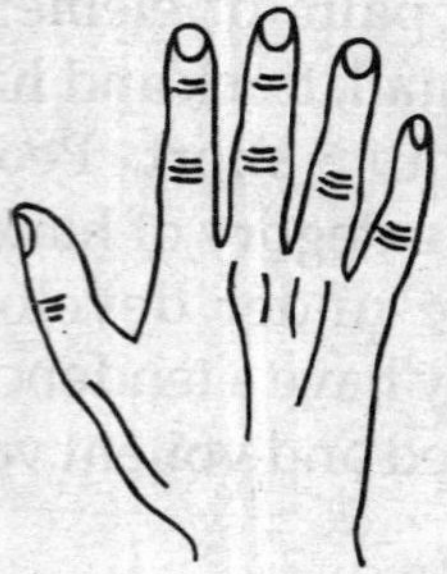

Fig. 1-d: Philosophic Hand

<u>Conical Hand</u> - See fig. 1 - e

The finger tips of conical hand are rounded. They are emotional people. Also, they are sensitive and intutive. The conical hand people are social and are fond of music and art. These people are sensitive to their surroundings.

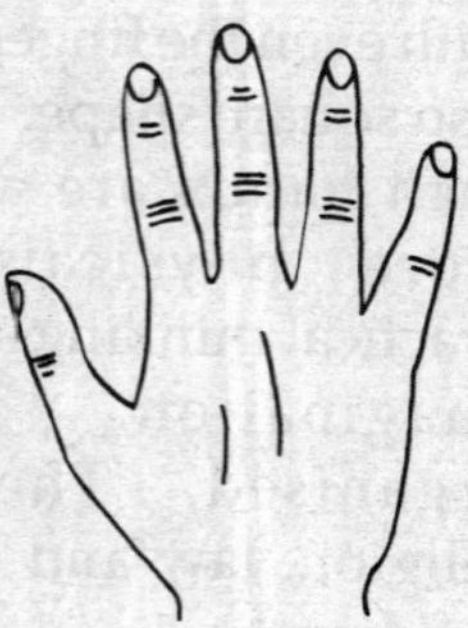

Fig. 1-e: Conical Hand

<u>*Psychic hand*</u> - See fig. 1 – f

The fingertips of psychic hand are pointed with soft knuckles. Those with psychic hand have limited working capacity and are not organised. They get inspired quickly and are too sensitive to be practical.

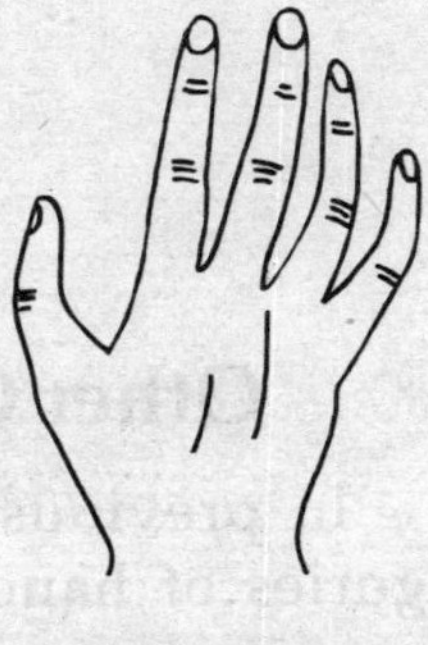

Fig. 1-f: Psychic Hand

<u>*Mixed hand*</u> - See fig. 1 – g

These hands have many peculiarities of of all the other types of hand. The fingers are not uniformly shaped. One can be conical the other might be pointed. Such a person has a versatile personality.

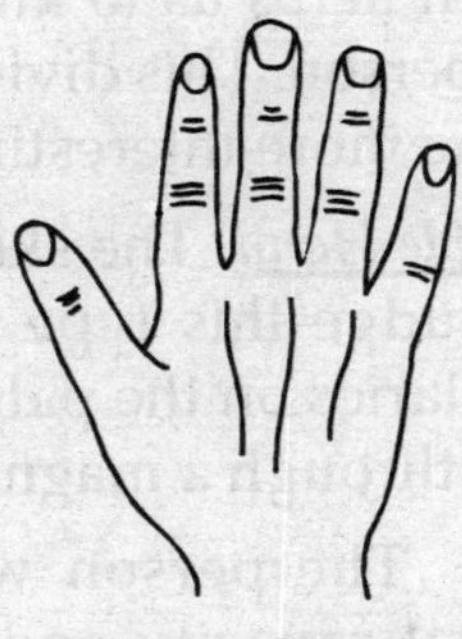

Fig. 1-g: Mixed Hand

Chapter – 7

Other Categories of Hand

In previous chapter, we have discussed the categories of hand according to French palmist – D' Arpentingny, but Prof. Dayanand (Head of Institute of Palmistry) acknowledges the other type of division, which helps us to know the nature and basic instincts of a person. This division has made palmistry easy and all the more interesting.

Flexible Hand The skin of hand is flexible and smooth. We judge this type of hand through fine pattern of capillaries on the palm which appear more clear when seen through a magnifying glass.

The person with flexible hand have greater mental capacity and is open minded. The owner of flexible hand is always ready to accept new ideas.

Firm hand The skin of firm hand is flexible and the palm is firm. People having firm hand have power of thought and action. They are logical and are good in making decision.

Hard Hand The skin of such a hand is rough. (The capillaries of their skin pattern can be seen without even a magnifying glass). Person with hard hand do not accept new idea easily and also have conservative outlook in making friends. People with hard hand are good workers.

Broad Hand Broad Hand has broad appearance and the fingertips are square. Owner of broad palm is pragmatic by nature with less imagination. They take quick decision and if their skin is flexible the quality of their work also improves.

Long Hand Long palm indicates a thoughtful inward turn of mind. People with long hand are good planners, and are often introvert. They have more mental power than physical. If the knots of fingers are prominent then they have a practical bent dominating their thinking.

Heavy Hand The palm of heavy hand is thick. People with heavy hand have more physical stamina and are couragious. They have greater capacity to work. If the skin of heavy hand is flexible then owners of such hand are inclined to be practical, steady with artistic bent of mind.

People with soft flabby hand are not hard workers. They have strong sexual urge and spend more time in merry making.

Thin Hand Palm of such people is on the thinner side with less flesh and muscle. Owners of such a hand are conservative, petty minded and less couragious.

Chapter – 8

The Thumb and Fingers

The Thumb

Every person has four fingers and one thumb and each finger contains three phalanges and two knots. The thumb has two phalanges and one knot. (See fig. 2 – a)

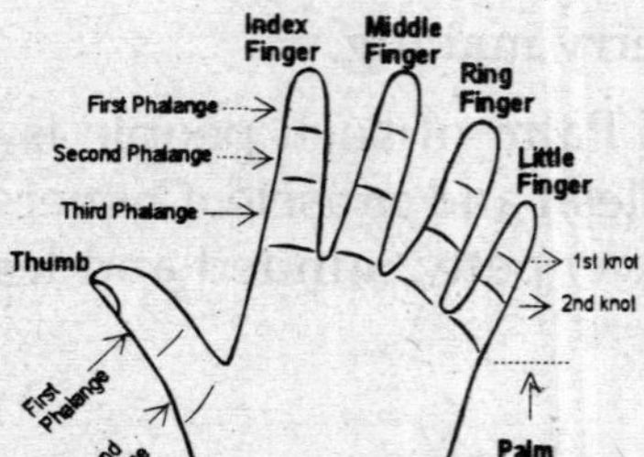

Fig. 2a

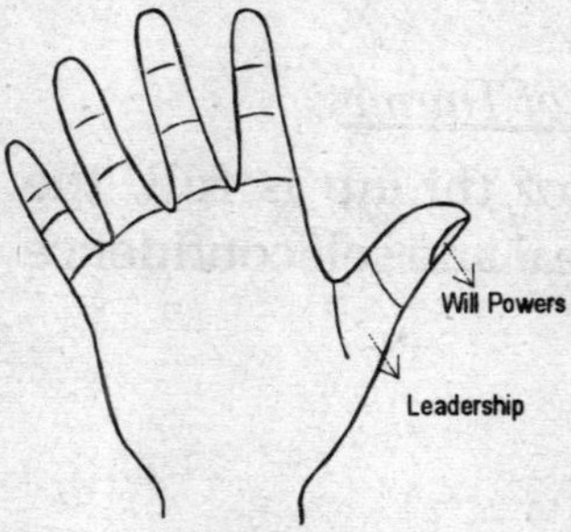

Fig. 2b

__The Thumb__

The thumb is the most important digit of our hand. It signifies intelligence and will power. It reveals determination, logical power and capacity of decision making of the individual.

The normal length of thumb indicates good mental faculty. Whereas the people with short thumb act instinctively and those with long thumb have lust for power.

__Parts of Thumb__ __(See fig. 2 – b)__

Thumb has two phalanges. The tip or first phalanges represents will power, leadership ability and efficiency to work.

If the first phalange is long the person is of firm resolve and man of action

The second phalange shows logic, tact, planning and reasoning ability of person. Persons with longer second phalange think more, but execute less.

Other Peculiarities of Thumb

If the tip of thumb is full, the person is full of zeal and self confidence (See fig. 2 – c)

Fig. 2c

If the tip of thumb is developed like a club, such a man is violent by disposition. (See fig. 2 – d) And if the tip of thumb is flat the man is likely to be stubborn. (See Fig. 2 – e).

Fig. 2d

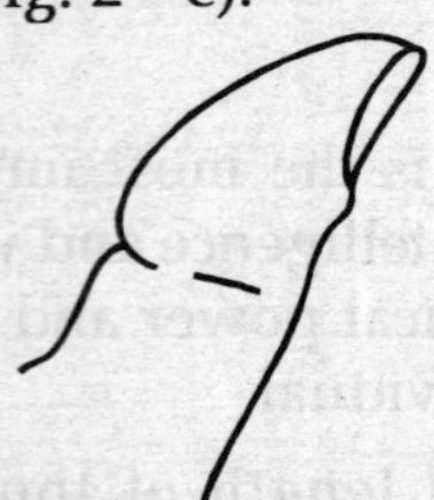

Fig. 2e

If the thumb is straight person is balanced, tactful, practical and open minded.

A thumb bending inward towards palm indicate violent personality whereas if it bends outwards the person is likely be social, warm and sympathetic.

Chapter – 9

The Fingers

The fingers are divided into three phalanges by two knots. The first phalange which contains nail on the back side and fingertips that represent the mental world. The middle or second phalange represents the practical world and the lower or third phalange represents the instinctive world. (See fig. 3).

The knot between first and second phalange is called first knot and the knot between second and third phalange is known as the second knot.

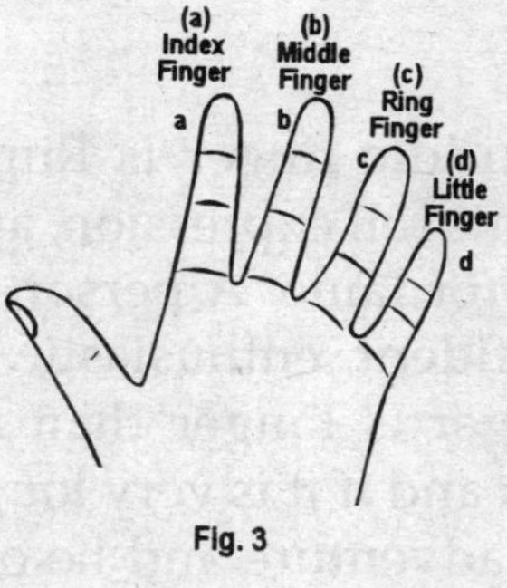

Fig. 3

The Index Finger

The first finger which is next to thumb is called Index Finger. It represents ego, leadership, desire for recognition and prestige. A longer Index Finger (longer than third finger) indicates desire for power and leadership. The person is egoistic and dominating.

A smaller then normal index Finger indicates lack of ambition and self confidence. The person will rather follow than lead.(See fig. 3 - a).

The Middle Finger

The finger next to index Finger is called middle finger or second finger. If the middle finger is longer than all other fingers then it is considered normal. It represents the balanced mind with sagacity and soberness. Very long middle finger indicate love for solitude. Such a person is not socialy active. He or she loves to remain alone.

Person having shorter than normal middle finger is petty minded and cares more for money. (See fig. 3 – b)

The Ring Finger

Next to middle finger is Ring Finger or third finger. It represents self expression, appreciation, social grace and desire for fame. A person with normal ring finger is self confident, enthusiastic and socialy more active. If the finger is longer than index Finger one enjoys taking risk and if it is very long the person takes much interest in adventure and he or she can indulge in games of chance. Shorter ring finger indicates less enthusiasm. (See fig. 3 – c)

The Little Finger

Though smallest in size Little Finger has greater importance in palmistry than any other finger. If it reaches the first knot of the Ring Finger it is considered to be of normal length. If it is below it, it is considered shorter.

Persons with normal little finger are good speakers and they are good in making new contacts. They can be good P.R.O. Their nervous system is well developed and they are intelligent.

The long little finger helps him or her in excelling in politics, trade, sciences etc. Person with short finger have contrary nature. They are generally introvert and they never reveal their mind.(See fig. 3 – d).

Chapter – 10

The Mounts on the Hand

Palmistry has divided the palm in nine zones. Each zone indicates some mental, physical peculiarities and characteristics of the individual. These zones are known as Mounts. (See fig. 4)

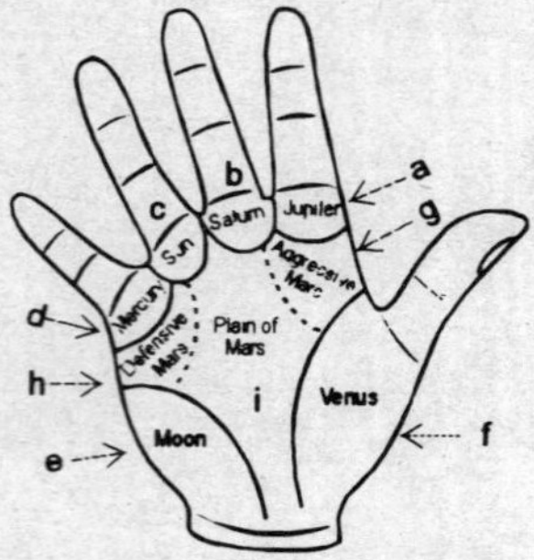

Fig. 4

These Mounts have been named after various planets. In some hands these Mounts are prominent and in other they may be flat. Those which are prominent are called developed Mounts. The flat or under developed Mounts are called suppressed Mounts.

<u>*The Mount of Jupiter*</u> - See fig. 4 – a

The Mount of Jupiter is at the base of Index Finger. Jupiter represents ambition, pride, loyalty, ego and ability to lead others.

Persons with developed Mount of Jupiter are ambitious, egoistic, honest and they follow certain ideals.

If the Mount of Jupiter is over developed, a person's ego turns into arrogance. Those with level or depressed Mount of Jupiter have no ambitions. The Index Finger has some qualities of Jupiter.

<u>*The Mount of Saturn*</u> - See fig. 4 - b

This Mount is at the base of second or middle finger. This Mount reflects sensitivity, sobriety, wisdom and analytical power of the person.

Persons with developed Mount of Saturn are sober, wise, serious and introvert. They are good planners and analysing things is part of their nature.

Long palm and long fingers tend to accentuate the qualities of Saturn whereas broad palm reduces its effect.

The Middle Finger represents the qualities of Mount of Saturn.

<u>*The Mount of Apollo or Sun*</u> - See Fig. 4 – c

The zone at the base of Ring Finger indicates desire of an individual to gain prominence. It also signifies hope, zeal, enthusiasm, desire for fame and tendency to show off.

A person with a prominent Jupiter has ambitions, but they are fulfilled only if the Mount of the Sun is also developed. Those with a prominent Mount of Sun have a happy disposition. They are open minded and take interest in arts. A person with an under developed Mount of the Sun has no desire for ostentation. The Ring Finger has some of the qualities associated with this Mount.

The Mount of Mercury - See Fig. 4 – d

Mount of Mercury is at the base of Little Finger, It indicates practical thinking, worldlywiseness & business ability. Mercury is associated with quick wit and fast talking. Persons with prominent Mount of Mercury are good speakers. They have natural affinity for the sciences. Mercurians can be very tactful and have a great deal of business sense. They don't believe in idealism.

Persons with an over developed Mount of Mercury are self centered. Persons with an under developed Mount of Mercury are simple and without any guile. The little finger has some of the qualities associated with this Mount.

Mount of Luna or Moon - See fig. 4 – e

Mount of Luna is at the side of Mount of Mercury close to the wrist. Luna indicates imagination, the power of divination and the faculty of intuition.

Person with developed Mount of Moon has strong desire for change and they love travelling. They have acute imagination and a restless disposition.

Mount of Venus - See fig. 4 – f

Mount of Venus is at the base of thumb. This Mount indicates physical vitality, libido or sexual power and generosity of a person. If this Mount is firm and spreads over an area wider than normal, the person is said to have prominent Mount of Venus. A normal development of the Mount of Venus makes a person healthy and optimist. Such persons maintain relations. They worship beauty and have sex appeal. They make friends easily and have a desire to live a happy life. An over developed Mount of Venus indicates excessive sexual urge.

A person with an under developed Mount of Venus suffers from a sense of insecurity. He or she lacks in physical strength.

Aggressive Mars - See fig. 4 – g

The area below Mount of Jupiter is called Aggressive Mars. It indicates courage, bravery and domination in a person. Persons with prominent Aggressive Mars are generally dominating.

Defensive Mars - See Fig. 4 – h

Defensive Mars is located below the Mount of Mercury and above the Mount of Moon. It indicates patience and resistance power. When both Mounts of Mars are developed the person has both aggression and resistive power.

Plain of Mars - See fig. 4 – i

The area between these two Mars and the Mounts of Venus and Luna is called Plain of Mars. The developed Plain of Mars indicates that person is full of physical energy and depressed Plain of Mars shows lack of physical energy and accentrated irritability.

Chapter – 11

Finger Prints

The first phalange of the finger and the thumb are the most sensitive parts of the digit. On the reverse side are the nails while the finger prints are taken of the palm side.

These finger prints are not clearly visible without magnifying glass and they differ in shapes. Finger prints reveal about person's health and mentality.

There are six types of finger prints.

Whorl (See fig. 5 – a)

A whorl normally indicates will power. If the numbers of whorls are more on the fingers, the person will not change his views easily and may be stubborn by nature.

Fig. 5a

<u>*Loop*</u> (See fig. 5 – b)

A loop is most commonly found sign. It is found in most of palms. Person with many loops are of adjustible nature, but they have poor digestive system.

Fig. 5b

<u>*Closed Loop*</u> (See fig. 5 – c)

Person with this pattern on finger tips are neither too stubborn nor too flexible. They are balanced people but this pattern is not very commonly found.

Fig. 5c

Arch (See fig. 5 – d)

More arches on finger indicate restless and impatient temperament. Person with more arches have a sensitive digestive system.

Fig. 5d

Tented Arch (See fig. 5 – e)

Tented Arches are found rarely. People with more Tented Arches have less tolerance. They appear always tensed up and can easily succumb to nervous disorder.

Fig. 5e

<u>*Composite Loop*</u> (See fig. 5 – f)

People having composite loop are not clear in their thoughts. They are not able to take quick decision and get nervous quickly.

Fig. 5f

<u>*A Mixed Pattern*</u>

Very few people have more patterns of the same kind. Generally they have mixed pattern on different fingers. In order to judge the temperament of a person the majority of patterns on fingers should be considered.

Chapter – 12

The Nails

Finger nails tells a lot about the man's health, his vital force and his disposition.

<u>*Colour and size of Nails*</u>

Pinkish nails indicates fine state of health and liberal disposition.

Red nails are the sign of excess of physical energy, anger and tendency towards violence.

White nails indicate hasty temperament and self centered nature.

Yellow nails reveals disorder of liver.

<u>*Size of a Nail*</u>

<u>*Large Nail*</u> - (See fig. 6 – a)

A nail which is long as well as broad, indicates a placid temperament and tactful nature. Person possessing large shiny nails has good physical and mental health.

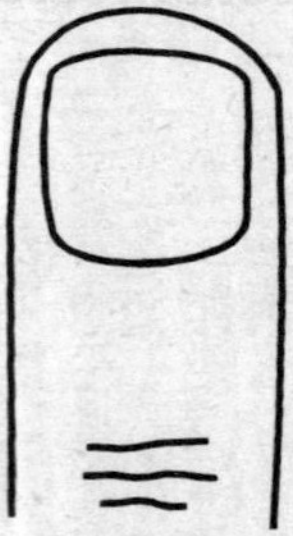

Fig. 6a

<u>*Small Nail*</u> - (See fig. 6 – b)

A small nail is more broad and it covers the whole breadth of fingers. Owner of a small nails has less tolerance. Such persons take quick decision and do not listen to others.

Fig. 6b

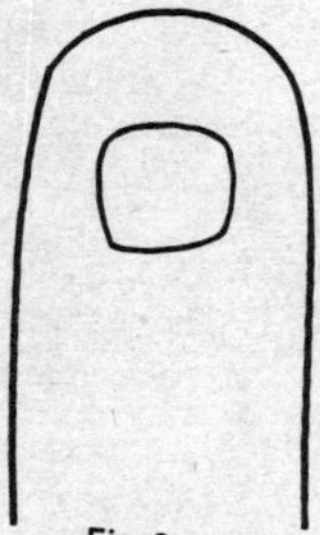

Fig. 6c

<u>*Very Small Nail*</u> (See fig. 6 – c)

Such nails are short both in length and width. They appears like a spot on a finger. These people are possessive about money matters.

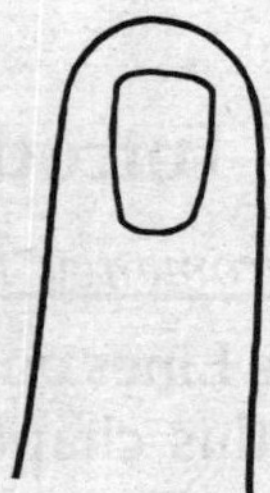

Fig. 6d

<u>*Long Nails*</u> (See fig. 6 – d)

These nails are full in length but short in width. Person with long nail are cool headed and artistic by nature but have less physical power. They are sensitive by nature and hence they get frustrated easily.

<u>*Vertical Lines on Nails*</u>

Vertical stripes on nails indicate weakness of nervous system. The more the stripes the greater mental stress.

<u>*Spot on Nails*</u>

White spots on the nail indicate mental tension. Yellow and black spots indicate ill health.

Chapter - 13

Chiromancy

Introduction of Lines on the Palm

Chiromancy is the study of Lines

The Lines on the Palm are divided into three categories. In this chapter we are introducing different kinds of lines. The descriptive details of these lines are given in forthcoming chapters. They are:-

1. Main Lines
2. Secondary Lines
3. Other Lines and Lines of influence

Main Lines

The Lines which are found on most of the hands are called main lines. There are three main lines, (See fig. 8)

(1) *The Life Line* - (See fig. 8 – a)

Life Line reveals about physical capacity, energy and family matters of the person.

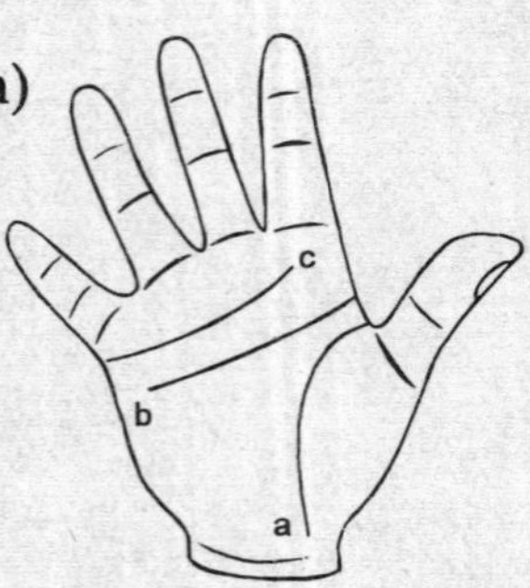

Fig. 8

(2) *The Head Line* - (See fig. 8 - b)

Head Line reveals about the mental capacity, memory and intelligence of a person.

(3) *The Heart Line* - (See fig. 8 – c)

Heart Line reveals about health, emotions and sensitivity of a person.

Secondary Lines - (See fig. 9)

These lines are not found in most of hands but they play very important role in the person's life.

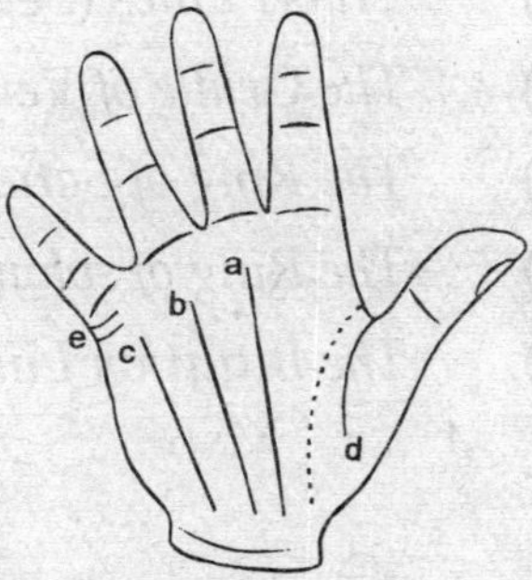

Fig. 9

(1) *Line of Saturn* - (See fig. 9 – a)

It is generally called line of fate and wealth. Line of Saturn reveals about struggle of life, carrier, financial gains and changes in life.

(2) *Line of Sun* - (See fig. 9 – b)

This is a supporting line to Line of Saturn and is generally called Line of Success or Line of Fortune.

(3) *Line of Mercury* - (See fig. 9 – c)

Line of Mercury is also called Line of Health or Hepatica. This line reveals about sharpness, intelligence and materialistic attitude of the person.

(4) *Line of Mars* - (See fig. 9 – d)

This is a parallel and supporting line to Life Line.

(5) *Marriage Line or Line of Sexuality* - (See fig. 9 – e)

This line is also called association line but we call it line of sexuality as it indicates sexual relationship of the individual with the opposite sex.

Other Lines

(1) *Line of Progeny or children* (See fig. 10 – a)

(2) *Travel Lines* (See fig. 10 – b)

(3) *The Gridle of Venus* (See fig. 10 – c)

(4) *The Ring of Saturn* (See fig. 10 – d)

(5) *The Ring of solomn* (See fig. 10 – e)

(6) *The Intuition Lines* (See fig. 10 – f)

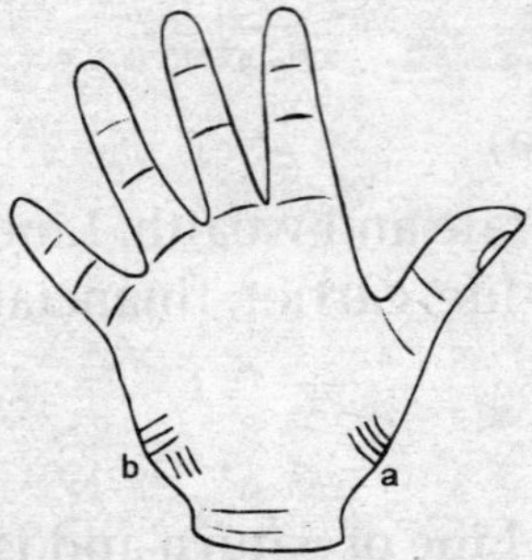

Fig. 10

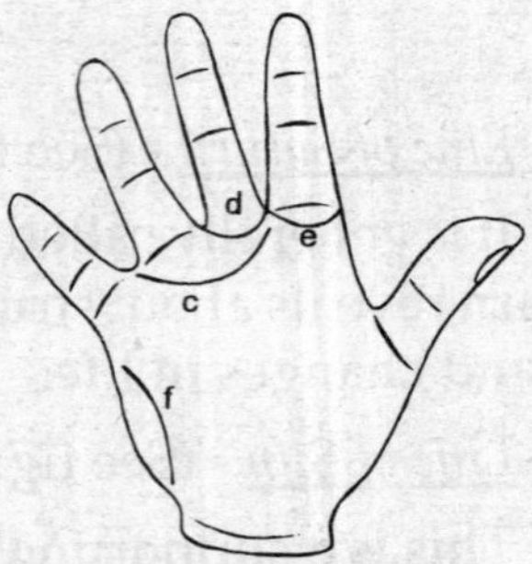

Fig. 10

Influence Lines or Chance Lines

These lines have no proper name but these lines influence our life in many ways and they also make contribution in forming different shapes and signs like cross , stars, triangle etc.

Quality of Lines

Thin and deep lines are best while shallow and broad lines are not good. The shallow and broad parts of a line indicate struggle and problems during that period.

The descriptive details of these lines are given in the forthcoming chapters.

Chapter – 14

Different Signs found on Hand

We have described in brief about the shapes of hand, fingers patterns of skin, nails and Mounts etc. in the previous chapters. Besides these there are many signs found on the palm. These shapes and signs are normally found on Mounts and Lines.

Many signs are formed due to the meeting of influence lines. All these lines indicate our fate to some extent, but their influence differ according to their placement on hand.

Here, we are describing different shapes and signs and their influence according to their placement.

<u>Cross</u> (See fig.11 - a)

A Cross is an auspicious sign if found on Mount of Jupiter. Cross on a Life Line indicates family problem. On Heart Line it indicates shock. If it is on Head Line this shows the possibilities of headache or short memory.

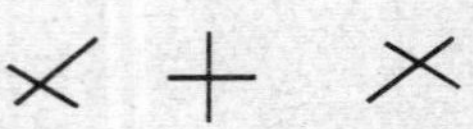

Fig. 11a- Cross

Star (See fig. 11 – b)

The effect of the presence of a star is good on Mount of Jupiter and Mount of Sun. The influence differs on other Mounts according to the quality of hand.

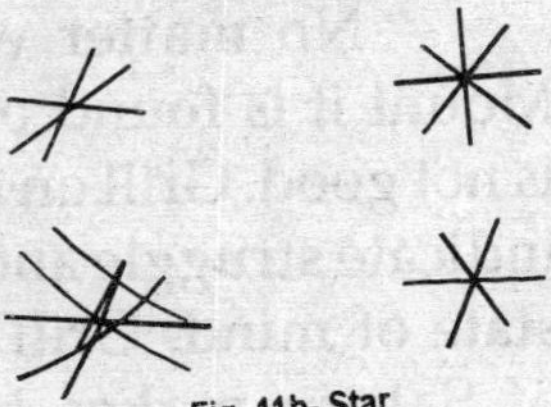

Fig. 11b- Star

A Star on Life Line indicates possible surgery. If it is at the end of short Head Line it indicates mental disorders. Star on Mount of Venus, Mount of Sun and on Mount of Aggressive Mars indicates headache.

Island (See fig. 11 – c)

Island is good if found on the Joint of phalanges of Thumb. This indicates financial security. Every where else it is bad.

If it is on Line of Saturn it indicates loss of wealth. An island on Sun Line shows blemish on person's name and fame.

Fig. 11c- Island

Triangle (See fig. 11 – d)

Triangle is a beneficial sign everywhere. It is a sign of creativity. When found directly on any Line it activates the lines higher qualities.

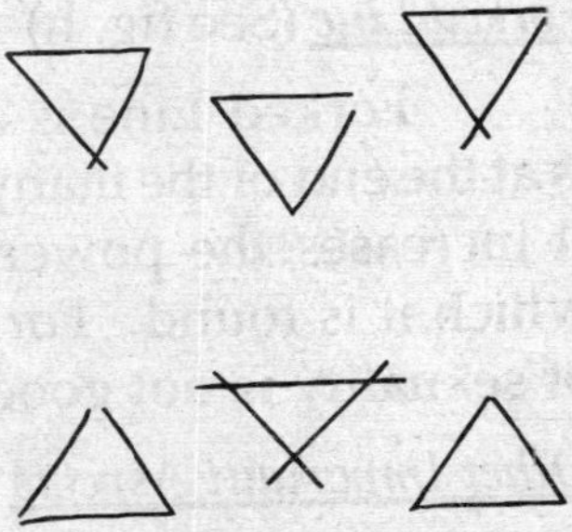

Fig. 11d- Triangle

Grill (See fig. 11– e)

No matter which ever Mount it is found on its effect is not good. Grill on any Mount indicate struggle and confused state of mind. Grill on Mount of Saturn makes brain over active.

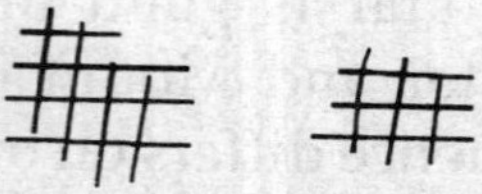

Fig. 11e- Grill

Trident (See fig. 11 – f)

Trident is usually found at the end of vertical line. It is beneficial if found towards finger and it reduces the energy and power of that line if found towards wrist.

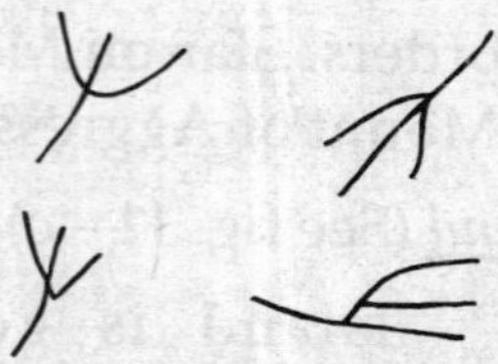

Fig. 11f- Trident

Tassel (See fig. 11 – g)

Tassel is usually found at the end of the line and it reduces the energy and influence of that line.

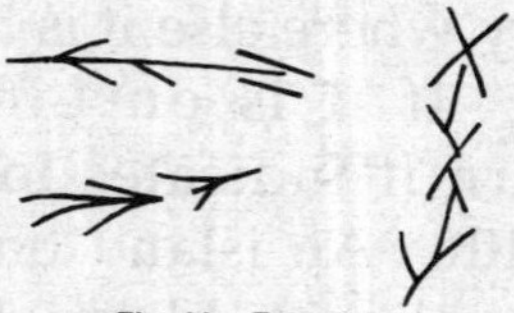

Fig. 11g- Tussel

Forked Line (See fig. h)

Forked Line is a good sign if it is at the end of the many secondry lines. It increases the power of that line on which it is found. Forked line on line of sexuality is not good.

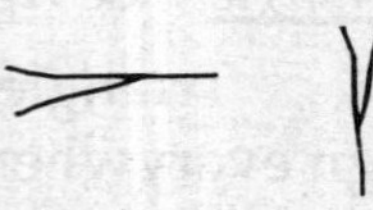

Fig. 11h

Other Important Aspects

Vertical Line : Vertical Lines generally have good effect but if there are more than two lines on Mount they reduce its effect.

Horizontal Line: Horizontal Lines generally considered obstructive, but not if they are on Mount of Venus. If these lines intersect the main lines they are called worry Lines.

Chapter - 15

How to calculate period of important events in Life

Every body wants to know about one's time of prosperity in one's life. Before we go further in detail of Lines we should know procedure of reckoning the time of good and bad events.

<u>Lines can only indicate the approximate time of an event</u>

<u>Reckoning events time from Life Line</u>

The Life Line indicates the physical capacity of the person. It originates between the Mount of Jupiter and Aggressive Mars and ends at wrist. The beginning part represents childhood, middle part for youth and ending part for old age. (See fig. - 12, age on the Life Line)

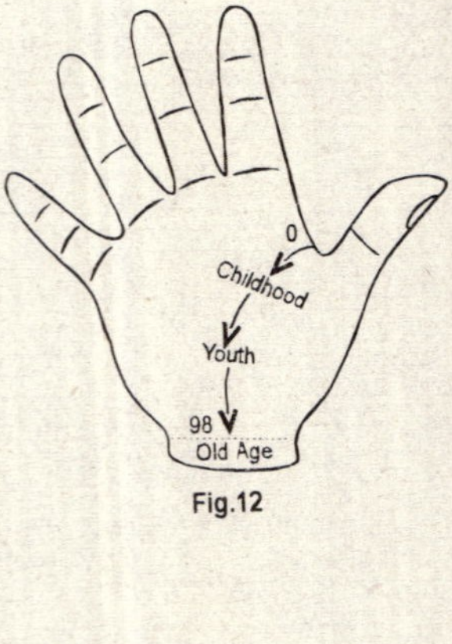

Fig.12

A simple method of marking the time on the Line of Life is to draw a line from the center of Mount of Venus, till the outer edge of the base of little finger. The point where the line intersects the Line of Life is reckoned as 35 years of age. (See fig. 12 – a)

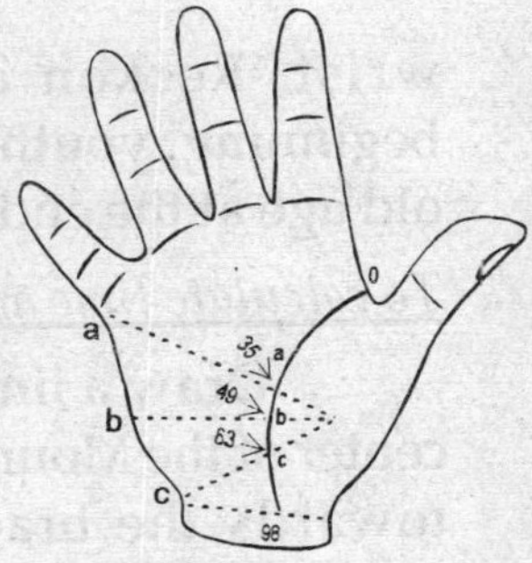

Fig. 12

Another horizontal line is drawn from the center of the Mount of Venus to the percussion (the outer edge of the palm towards Mount of Moon) and the point at which it intersects the Line of Life is 49 years of age. (See fig. 12 – b)

Draw third line from center of the Mount of Venus to the bracelet. The point at which this line intersects the Line of Life is 63 years of age. (See fig. 12 – c)

The point from where the Life Line begins age is reckoned as 0 years and the point where Life Line ends near wrist the age is reckoned 98 years. (See again fig. 12)

After understanding the life span from o to 98 and three major ages points (35, 49, 63) . It will be easy to mark other points for different ages.

Other rules Governing the Forecast of Progress, Profit and Carrier Prospects

Line of Saturn

If you look at fig. 13 , you would find a vertical line. It is Line of Saturn. It originates from wrist and ends at the base of Middle finger. Childhood events can be calculated from the beginning of the line near

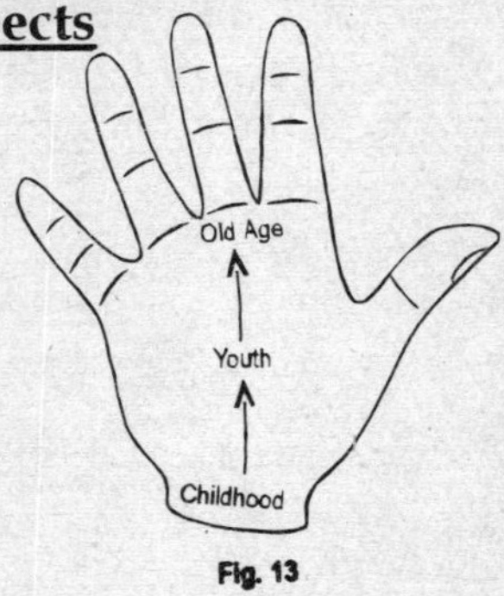

Fig. 13

wrist. Reckon childhood at the beginning, youth at the middle and old age at the end of line. (See fig. 13)

<u>*To calculate time and age*</u>

Draw a line from the center of the Mount of Venus towards the bracelet. The point at where the line intersects is 21 years of age. (See Fig. 13-1a)

Draw another line from the same point to the base of little finger. The point at the Line of Saturn intersects is 35 years. (See fig. 13 – 1c)

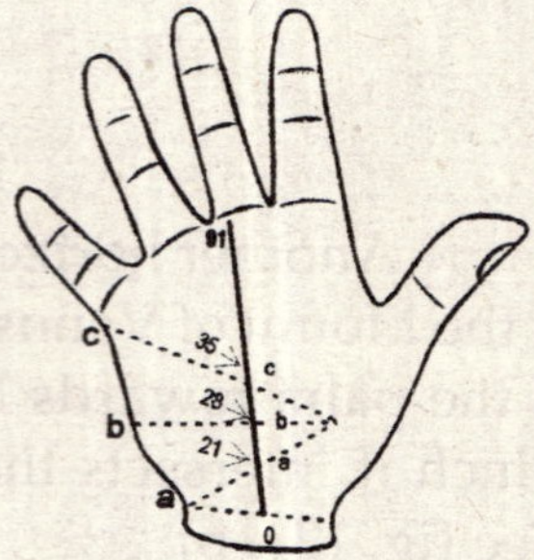

Fig.13-1

Draw third line from the center of the Mount of Venus to the percussion (other end of palm). The point where it intersects the Line of Saturn is 28 years. (See fig. 13 – 1b)

The beginning of line (from the wrist) is '0' years and the end (at the Mount of Saturn) is 91 years. In between these points (0, 21, 28, 35, 91) one can mark points for different ages.

Chapter – 16

The Line of Life

Life Line is a semi circular shape. It comes under main lines. It indicates about physical capacity, energy and family matters of a person.

<u>*Prediction by origin of Life Line*</u>

If the Life Line originates from Mount of Jupiter the person is ambitious and if the other signs are favourable he attains his ambitions. (See fig. 14)

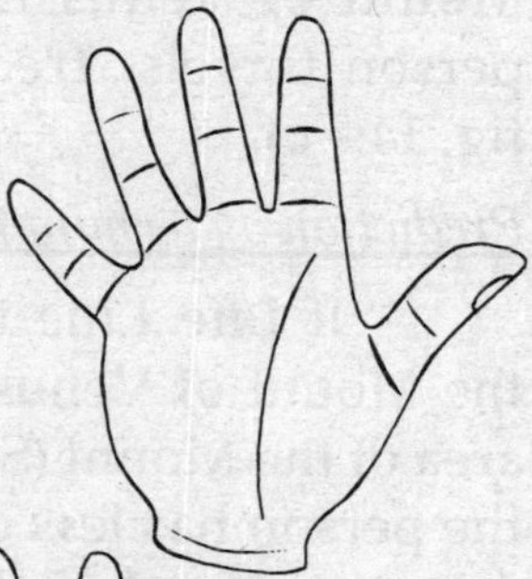

Fig. 14

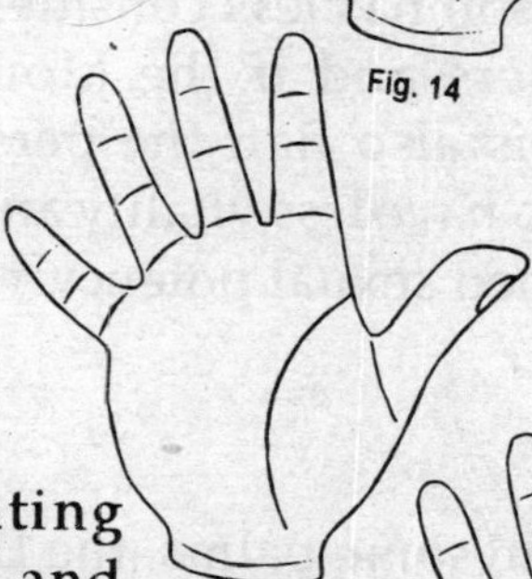

Fig. 14a

Life Line originating between Aggressive Mars and Mount of Jupiter shows balanced thinking of mind (See fig. 14 – a). But if line starts from the Aggressive Mars, he is sure to be aggressive in his behaviour. (See fig. 14 – b).

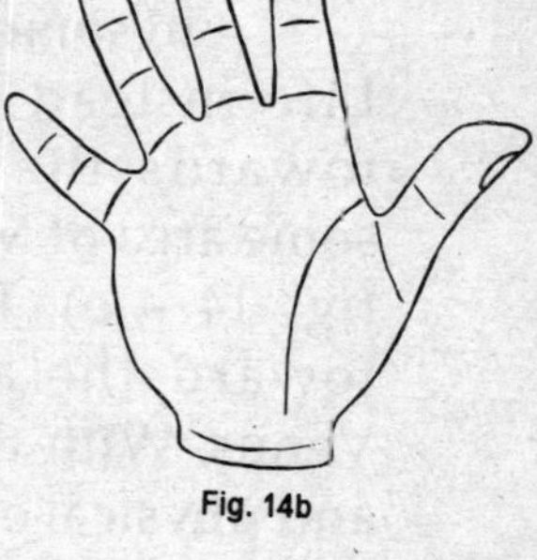

Fig. 14b

Life Line also indicates about abroad settlement and travelling

Line of Life reveals a lot about one's setting abroad and about travelling. If the Line of Life splits at the end into two branches, one going towards Mount of Venus and other one at Mount of Moon and if the branch going towards Mount of Moon is deep, the person settles abroad and if the branch going towards Mount of Venus is deeper the person travels frequently. (See fig. 14 – c).

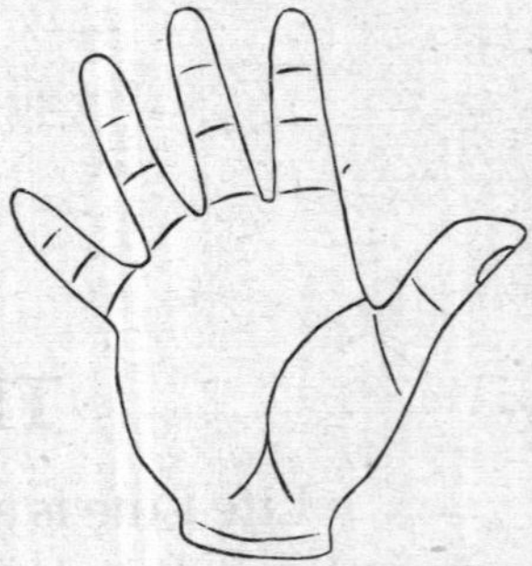
Fig. 14c

Prediction by termination of the line

If Life Line terminates at the Mount of Venus limiting the area of the Mount (See fig. 14 – d) the person has less consideration for others and if the Mount of Venus is also flat, the person is likely to have less vitality and also weakened sexual potency.

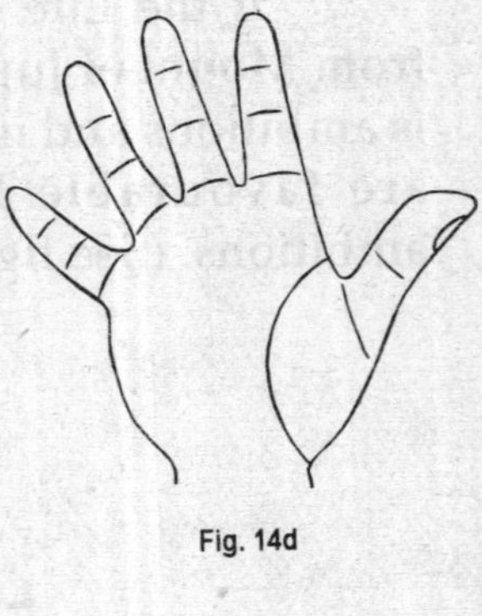
Fig. 14d

In some palms, the Line of Life instead of going straight towards the wrist envelopes some area of Mount of Moon (See fig. 14 – e). It tends to extend toward the area of Mount of Venus. With the result, sexuality and physical energy in the person also increases proportionately.

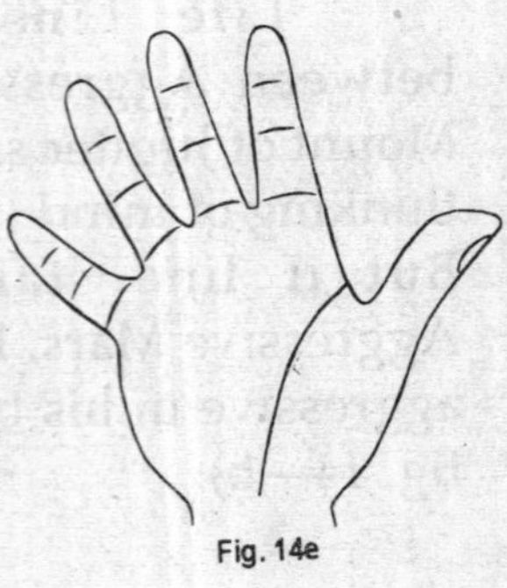
Fig. 14e

Other facts about Line of Life

Presence of an Island on Life Line is not considered good. This indicates health and family problems. A broken and chained line reveals struggle and problems.

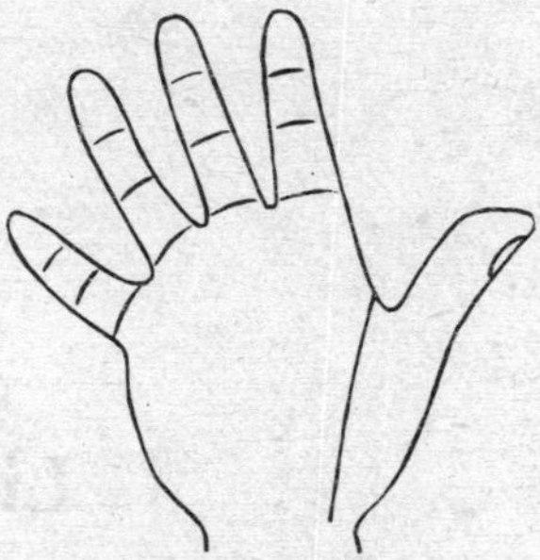

Fig. 14-f

A Shallow Life Line indicates weak health. Double Life Line indicates good health and straight Life Line (See fig. 14 – f) indicates more struggle.

Short Life Line does not show short life but it reveals monetary, family problem during that period. We can calculate the time of that period by the scale of Life Line.

Before predicting age of a person see both hands and other signs. If the line is short in both the hands and there is cross at the end of Line of Life, then it can indicates serious health problem.

Chapter - 17

Line of Head

Our brain controls our nervous system and the Line of Head represents precisely this delicate and intricate part of our body.

The Head Line indicates about the mental capability and intelligence of the person. It speaks about our ability of taking good or bad decisions. It is the most important line among the main lines of palm. If the head line is good it could mitigate the negative aspects of other lines but if it is defective, there is a possibility of its bad effect influencing other lines also.

Normally we see Line of Saturn to find out financial status, Line of Sun for success in life but I advise to study Head Line also, before reaching the final conclusion.

Prediction through the origin of Line of Head

Normally Head Line originates between Mount of Jupiter and Aggressive Mars. A thin deep Head Line indicates excellent brain and good memory (See fig. 15). Defective Head Line means mental problems and indecisive nature.

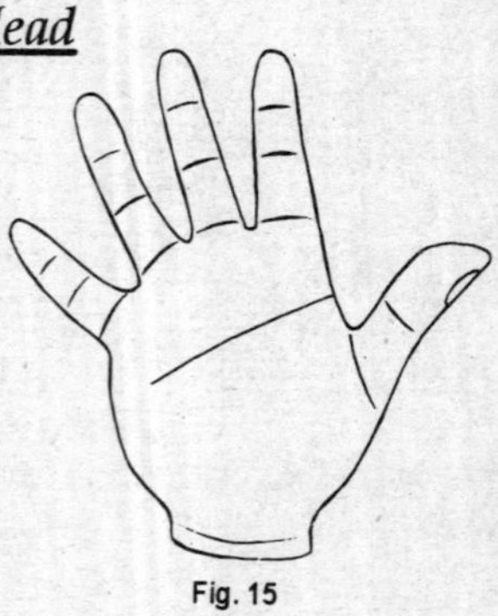

Fig. 15

If the Head Line separates after slightly touching the Life Line in the beginning (See fig. 15-a) and proceeds toward Defensive Mars, it reveals practical thinking and a good common sense. If it gets inclined towards Mount of Moon it indicates good imaginative power. (See fig. 15 – b).

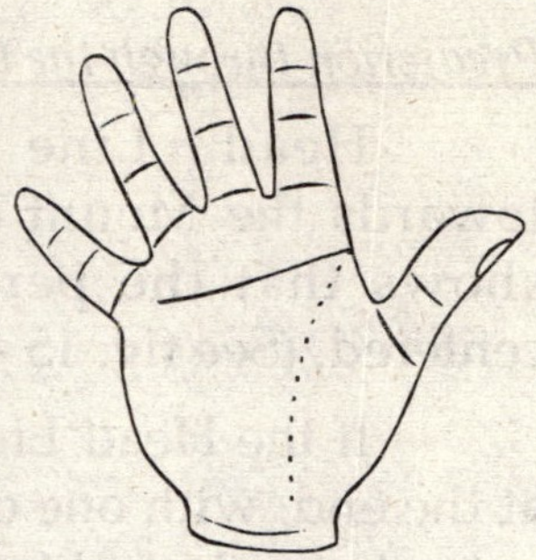

Fig. 15a

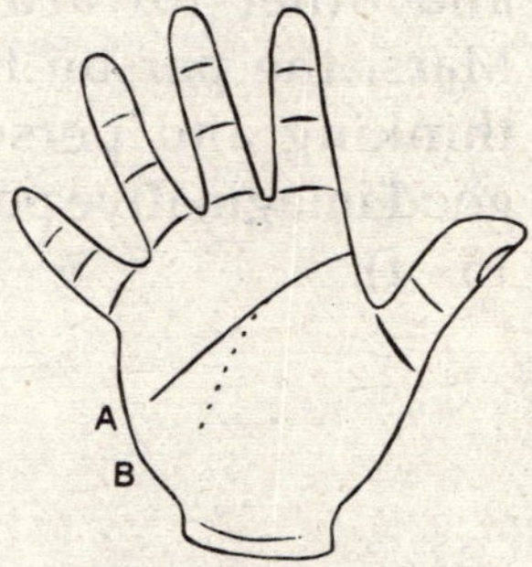

Fig. 15b

The Head Line originating at a distance from Life Line reveals that the person is carefree. He does not listen to others. (See fig. 15 – c).

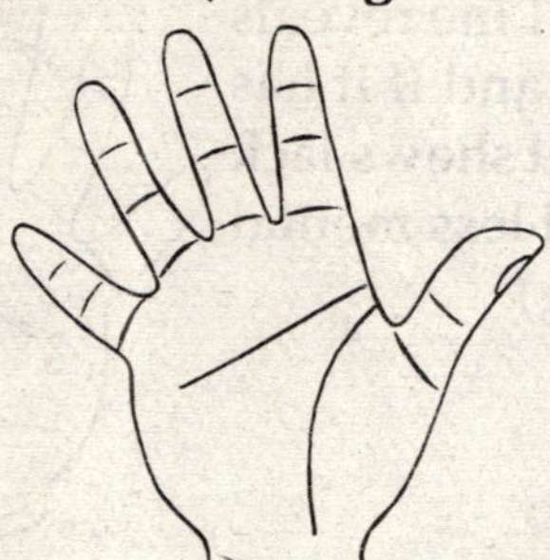

Fig. 15c

If the Head Line originates from the Aggressive Mars he or she is likely to be violent . (See fig. 15 – d)

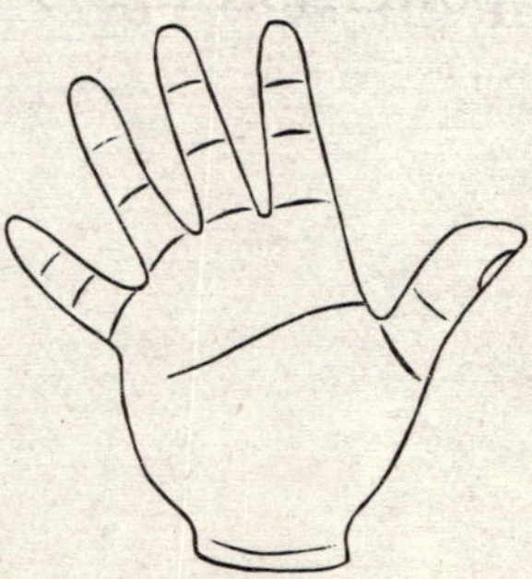

Fig. 15d

Prediction through the termination of Line of Head

Head Line inclining towards the Mount of Mercury shows that the person is self centered. (See fig. 15 – e).

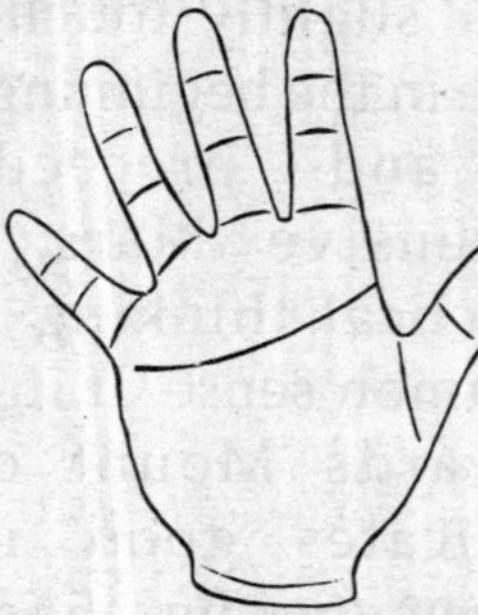

Fig. 15e

If the Head Line forks out at the end, with one of its branch going towards the Mount of Moon and other towards Defensive Mars, the person has balanced thinking and personality with good imaginative power. (See fig. 15 – f).

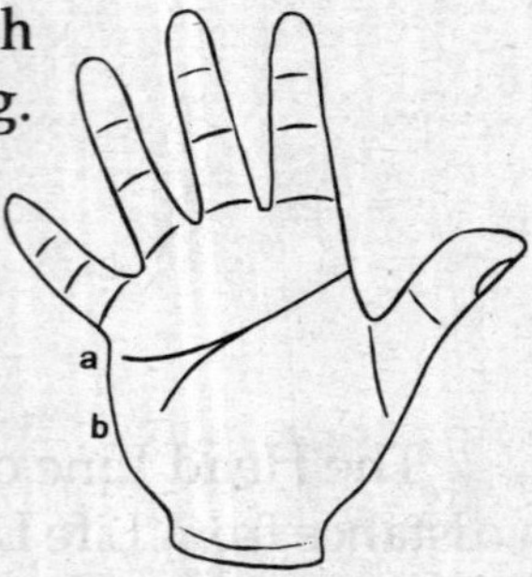

Fig. 15f

Other facts about Head Line

Shallow Head Line reveals lack of concentration and if it has tassel at the end then it shows lack of common sense and less mental power. (See fig. 15 – g).

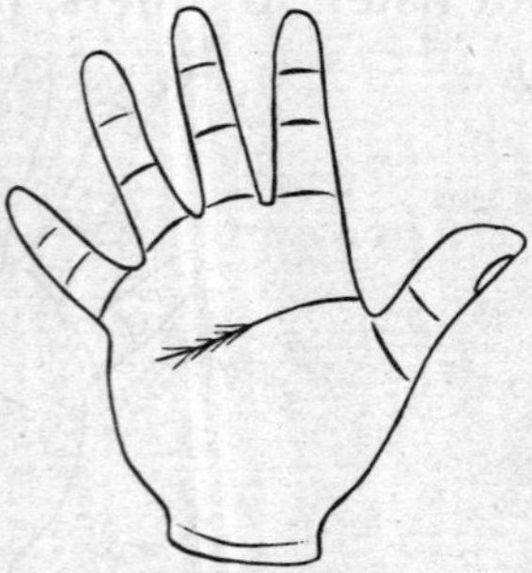

Fig. 15g

Chapter - 18

The Line of Heart

The Heart Line shows degree of sympathy and compassion the person possesses. It represents the sentimental status of emotions, feelings and health of a person. Their sentiments can be love, consideration for others, friendship, enmity, jealousy etc. All these sentiments depends on how sensitive a person is. Heart Line also reveals about our very important body organ the Heart. Health problems related to our sensitivity like tension and depression can also be measured by Heart Line. (See fig. 16)

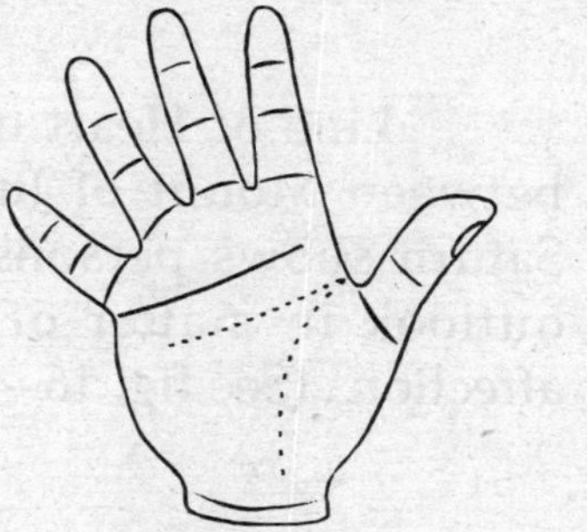

Fig. 16

Long and deep Heart Line indicates affectionate person; short and incomplete Heart Line reveals less sympathy, a selfish person, who thinks more about himself. And if the line is missing altogether then the person has no sentimental and emotional affinity for anyone.

<u>*Prediction through the origin of Line of Heart*</u>

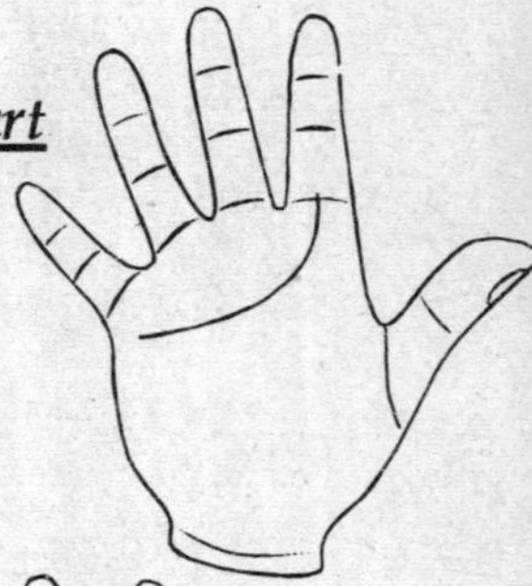

Fig. 16a

If the Heart Line originates from the third phalanges of Index finger the person is hypertensive. (See fig. 16 – a) He takes all the sentiments like love, hatred and jealousy with extreme sensitivity.

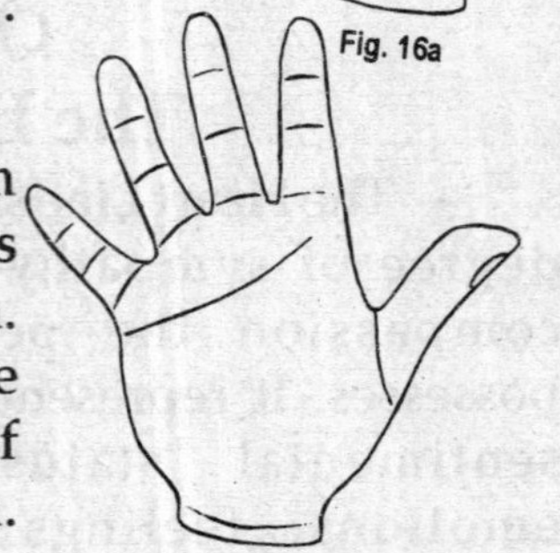

Fig. 16b

Heart Line starting from Mount of Jupiter indicates affectionate and liberal person. Such persons strive for ideal love and physical aspects of love is of secondary importance for them. (See fig. 16 – b)

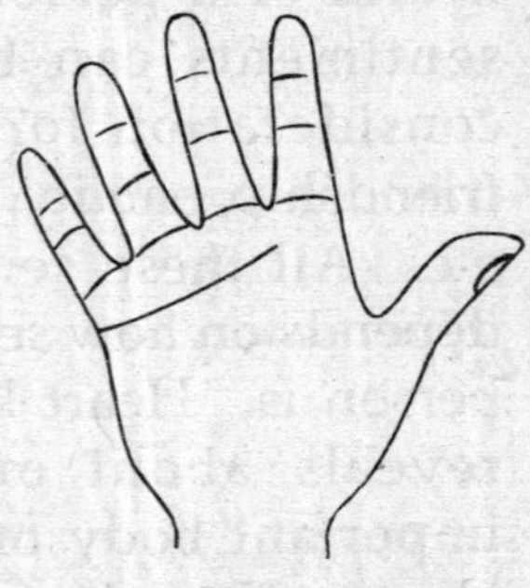

Fig. 16c

Line of Heart originating between Mount of Jupiter and Saturn shows persons practical outlook in matter of love and affection . (See fig. 16 – c).

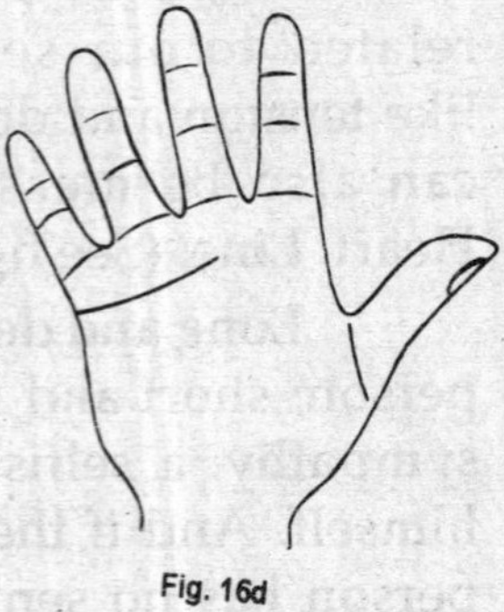

Fig. 16d

If the Heart line originates from Mount of Saturn the person is generally less sympathetic. His or her love is for his or her own pleasure. (See fig. 16 - d)

Other facts about Heart Line

The trident at the beginning of the Heart Line indicates balanced mentality. (See fig. 16 – e).

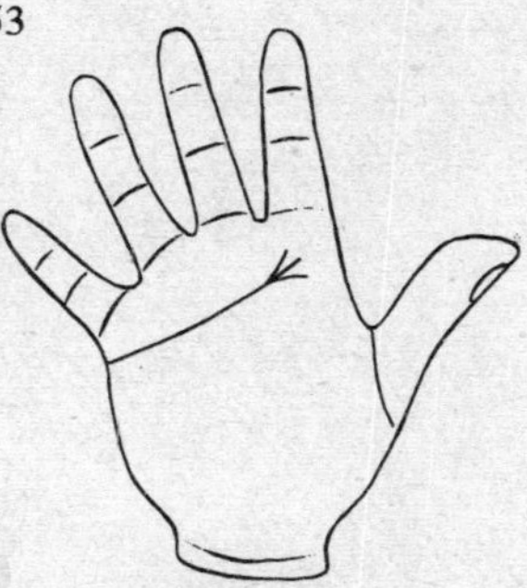

Fig. 16e

Broken and chained Heart Line indicates emotional and sentimental shocks and set backs, Heart Line with island indicates weakness of heart. (See fig. 16 – f)

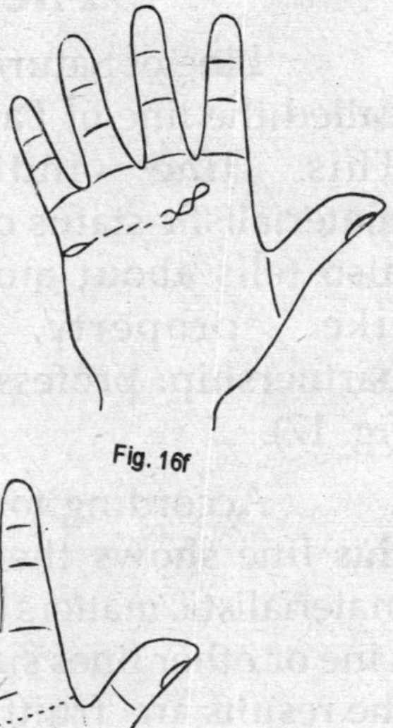

Fig. 16f

The closer the Heart Line runs to the base of the fingers (See fig. 16 – g), the more sentimental the person is, and if it is nearer to Head Line, more practical the person is likely to be.(See fig. 16 – h).

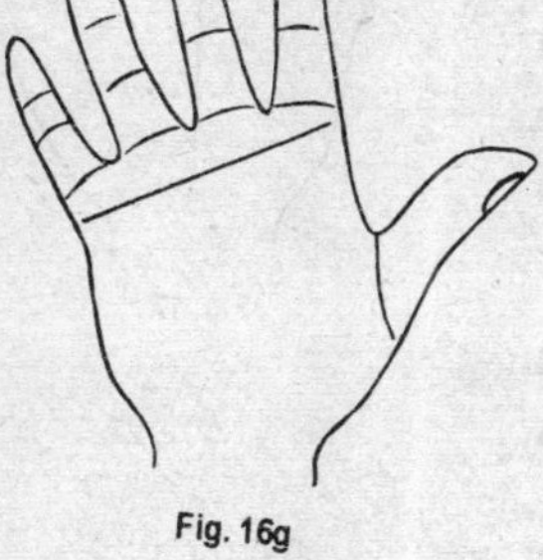

Fig. 16g

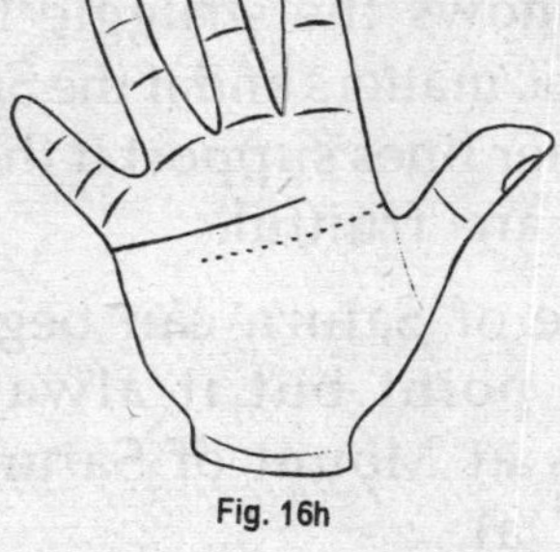

Fig. 16h

Chapter - 19

The Line of Saturn

Line of Saturn is generally called the line of Fate or Wealth. This line indicates the materialistic status of a person. It also tells about money matters like property, business, partnership, profession etc. (See fig. 17).

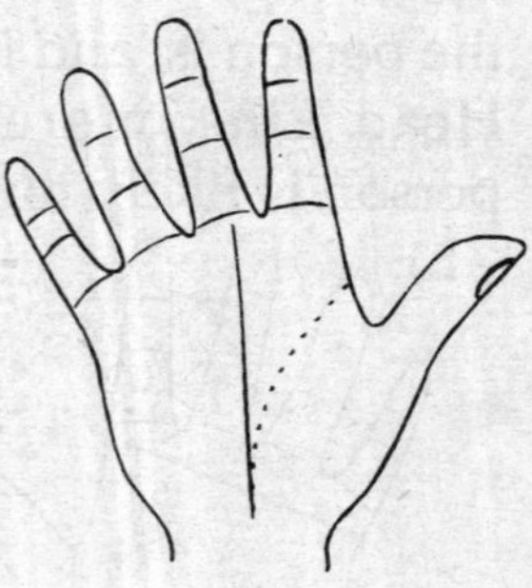

Fig. 17

According to our research this line shows the struggle for materialistic matters and if the Sun Line or other lines support it then the results are fruitful.

Line of Saturn can begin from any point but it always terminates at Mount of Saturn. (See fig. 17 a)

Origin

1) The Line of Saturn may originate from: wrist. (See fig. 17 – a – 1).

2) Mount of Moon (See fig. 17 – a – 2),

3) Line of Life (See fig. 17 – a – 3).

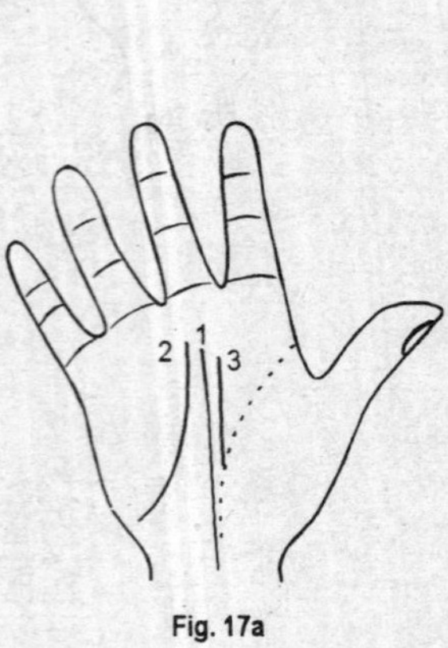

Fig. 17a

Prediction through the study of Line of Saturn

Line of Saturn emanating from wrist and going straight towards Mount of Saturn without touching the Life Line indicates smooth financial status. Such people have clear and definite goal in life. (See fig. 17 – b).

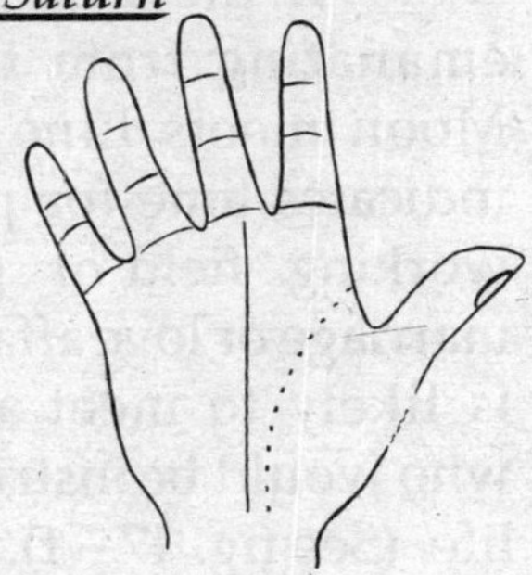

Fig. 17b

Line of Saturn emerging from Mount of Moon shows desire for worldly goods earned through fair means. (See fig. 17 – c)

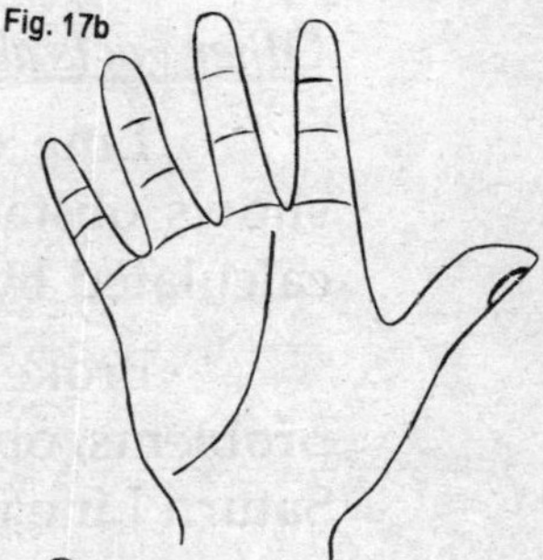

Fig. 17c

Line of Saturn starting from Life Line reveals that the person's identity will manifest truly when it branches off from the Life Line and goes towards the Mount of Saturn. The age can be calculated by the scale of Line of Saturn explained before. (See fig. 17 – d).

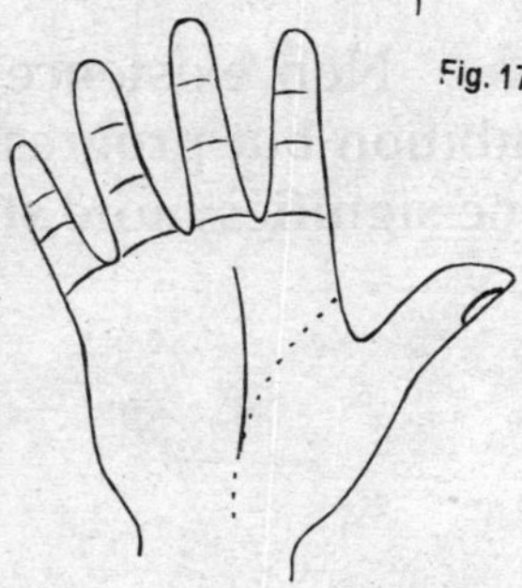

Fig. 17d

Saturn Line starting from Mount of Venus or from inside the Life Line indicates that a person gets burdened with family responsibilities in his youth only. (See fig. 17 – e)

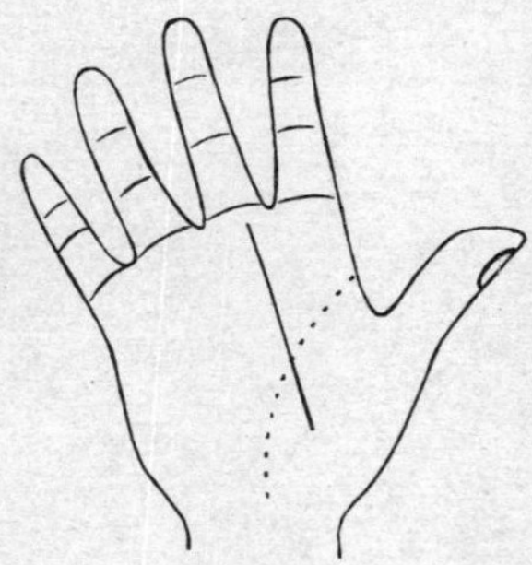

Fig. 17e

If the Line of Influence emanating from the Mount of Moon meets Line of Saturn, it indicates time for partnership in working field or good time for marriage or love affair. The person is likely to meet an individual who would be instrumental in his life. (See fig. 17 – f).

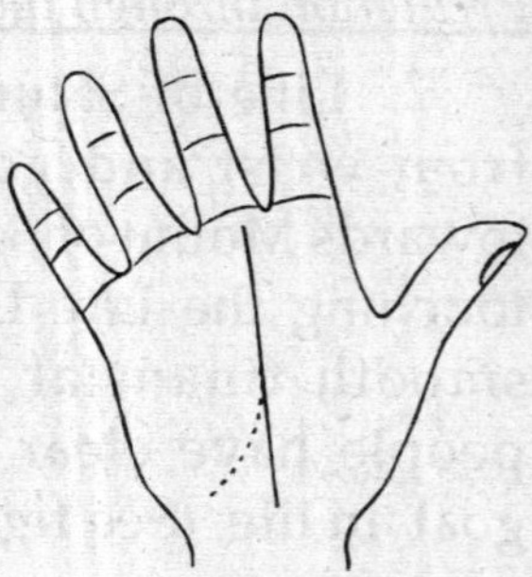

Fig. 17f

Other Facts about Line of Saturn

Line of Influence intersecting Line of Saturn shows obstacles at the age. The time period can be calculated by scale of Saturn Line.

Broken/shallow/chained Saturn Line indicates problems, obstacles and struggle at that age. Island on Saturn Line indicates obstacle in financial matters.

Non existence of Saturn Line signifies lack of ambition but progress in a routine way. Thick Saturn Line signifies more struggle and less gain.

Chapter - 20

The Line of Sun

Line of Sun is also called Line of Success. It is a supporting line to the Saturn Line. Sun Line brings luck. If there is Sun Line on palm one gets benefits and fruitful results in all walks of life whether the endeavour is for property, marriage, love, job, business or whatever. (See fig. 18)

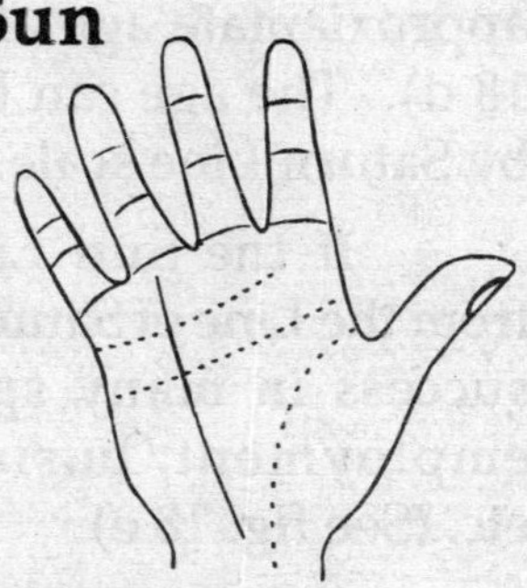

Fig. 18

<u>*Origin*</u>

The Sun Line may originate from –

1) Wrist (See fig. 18 – a1)

2) Mount of Moon (See fig. 18 – a2)

3) Line of Saturn (See fig. 18 – a3)

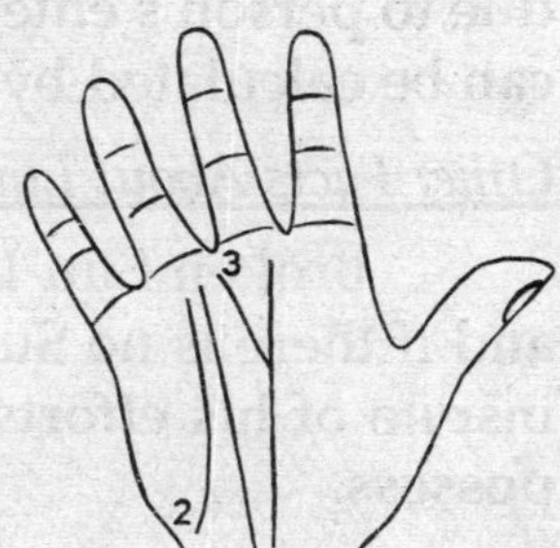

Fig. 18a

It can start from any point of hand but it always ends at Mount of Sun.

<u>*Prediction Through Origin of Line of Sun*</u>

Sun Line starting from wrist indicates success from early childhood. (See fig. 18 b).

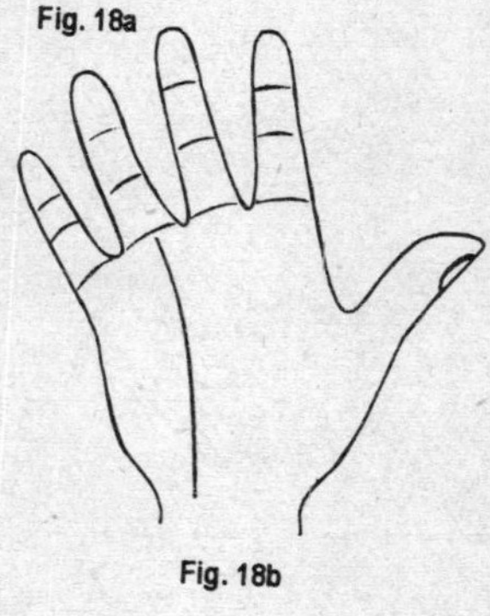

Fig. 18b

Sun Line starting from the middle of the palm signifies success at youth and if it originates from Head Line, it shows success through clear and good decision (See fig. 18 c). Sun Line starting from Heart Line shows success at the approxiamate age of 55. (See fig. 18 d). The age can be calculated by Saturn Line scale.

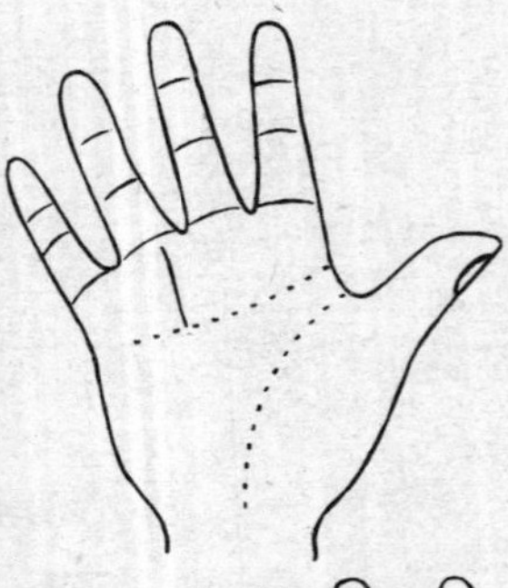

Fig. 18c

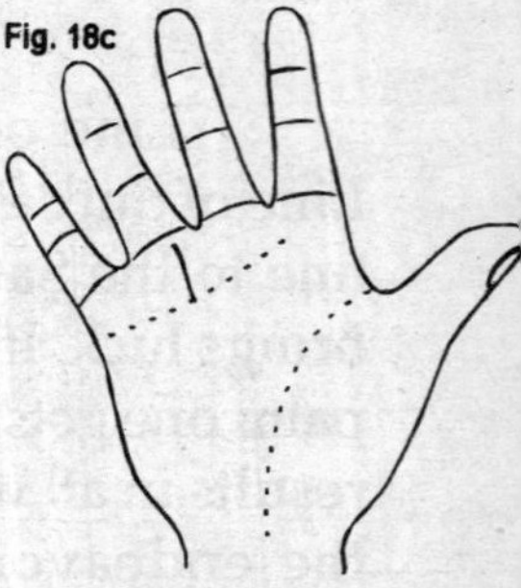

Fig. 18d

If the Sun Line emerges from the Line of Saturn it indicates success in many spheres like/ employment/ business/career etc. (See fig. 18 e)

A Sun Line starting from Life Line reveals success due to person's enterprising spirit and ability. The age can be calculated by Saturn Line scale.

Other Facts About Line of Sun

Broken Sun Line indicates temporary success, and if there is no Sun Line a person does not get fame inspite of his efforts and despite the talents he might possess.

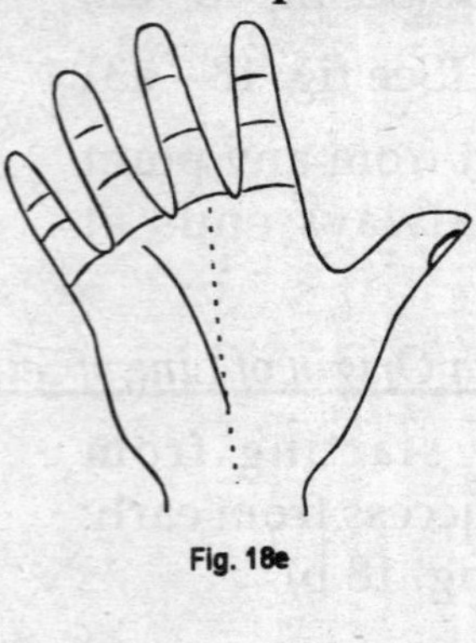

Fig. 18e

Chapter - 21

Line of Mercury

In Indian ancient sciences (*Samudrika shastra*) Line of Mercury is called *Swasthya Rekha* and western palmist call it Line of Health or Hepatica (Line of Liver). But according to the research of Prof. Dayanand, this line shows practical attitude of the person (See fig. 19).

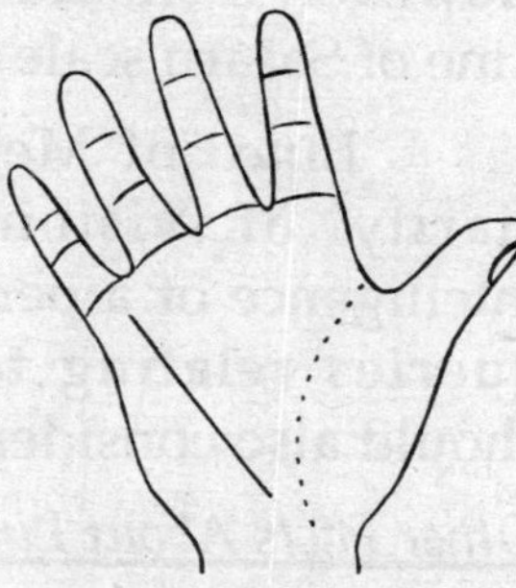

Fig. 19

Origin

Mercury Line may originate from

1) Line of Life (See fig. 19 – a1)

2) Mount of Venus (See fig. 19 –a2)

3) Mount of Moon (See fig. 19 – a3)

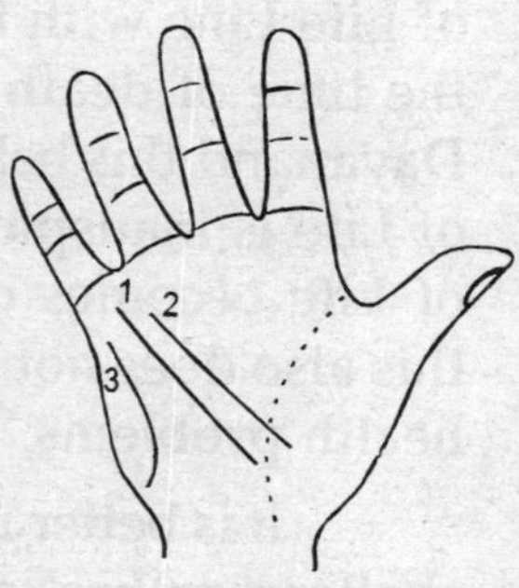

Fig. 19a

From where ever it may begin, it always ends at Mount of Mercury.

Prediction Through the Study of Line of Mercury

A well defined Line of Mercury starting from Mount of Moon indicates Travel and good business acumen. (See fig. 19 -b)

Line of Mercury emerging from Mount of Venus and intersecting Life Line signifies

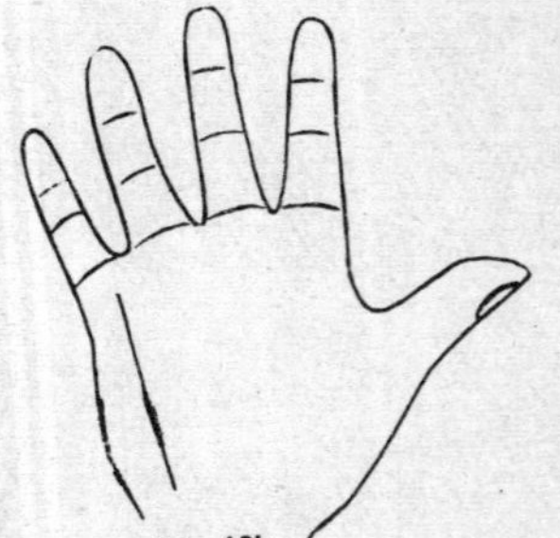

Fig. 19b

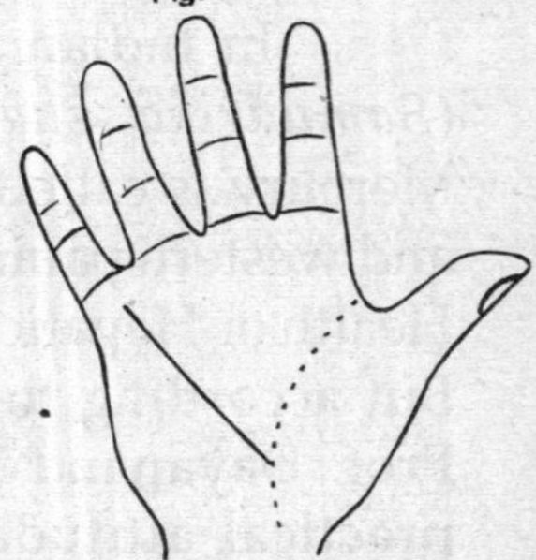

Fig. 19c

financial responsibilities till that point of age at which the line branches off from the Line of Life and moves towards the Mount of Mercury, since at that age the person business acumen and pragmatism starts showing better effect. However, it should be reckoned by Line of Saturn scale (See fig. 19 - c)

Line of Mercury signifies clarity of vision, health and intelligence of a person. To answer queries relating to business we should also consider Line of Saturn.

Other Facts About Line of Mercury

Some Western palmists believe that intersection of Life Line with that of the Line of Mercury indicates the time of death of a person. But according to Prof. Dayanand this belief is erroneous. Its touching the Line of Life is inauspicious only if after that point the Line of Life becomes defective or vanishes altogether. But this also does not predict death time; instead, it reveals health problems.

It is better not to have Mercury Line than to have shallow or broken line. Deep Mercury Line shows business and political acumen. Broken and wavy Mercury Line indicates digestive and liver problems. Absence of the Mercury Line indicates carefree nature of a person.

Chapter – 22

The Lines of Association / Sexuality and Marriage

Horizontal lines at the outer edge of Mount of Mercury are called Marriage Lines. In Western palmistry they are called Lines of Association and we call them Line of Sexuality. (See fig. 20)

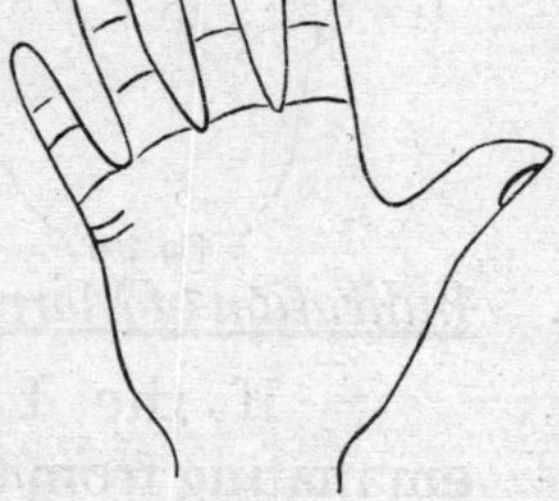

Fig. 20

Our experience and research tells us that these lines indicate less about marriage and more about sexual vitality of a person. To answer questions about marriage, other Lines on the palm should also be studied in addition to these lines. Detail is given ahead.

Prediction Through Marriage Lines

A single line of Marriage indicates attraction for opposite sex. Two such lines indicate that the sexuality would endure for a long time.

Straight and well defined lines signifies that the person is passionate and loves his spouse or sex partner dearly.

While giving answer to the question about marriage and love, line of Saturn and Mount of Moon should also be considered.

If the Line of Sexuality is inclined towards Heart Line (See fig. 20 a) it indicates ill health of spouse or quarrels in the couple.

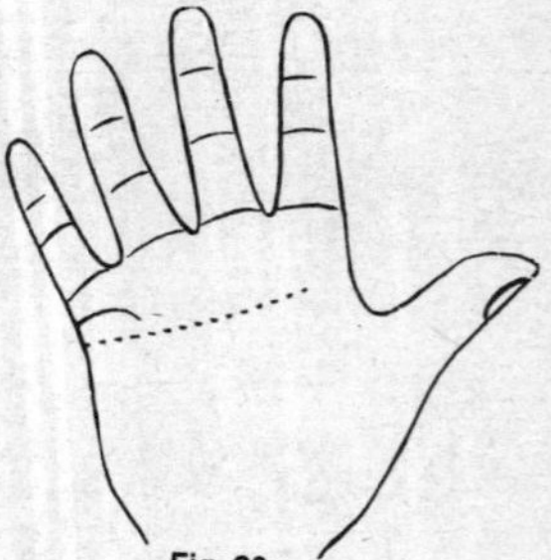

Fig. 20a

If the sexuality line intersect the Heart Line the person will have longer life than his spouse (See fig. 20 -b). If there is a break in the Line of Sexuality there is tendency to live away from ones spouse. (See fig. 20 -c)

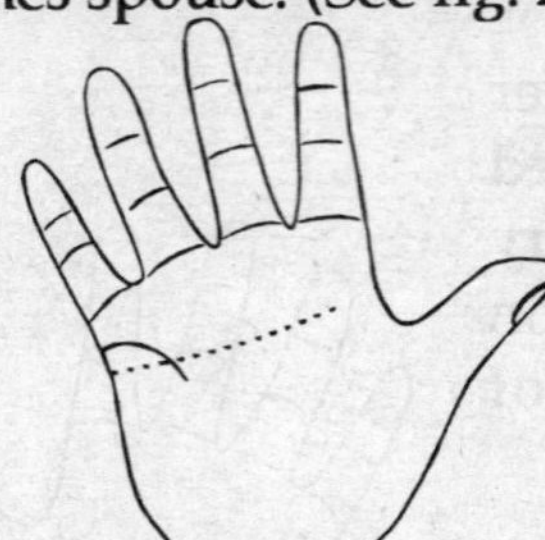

Fig. 20b

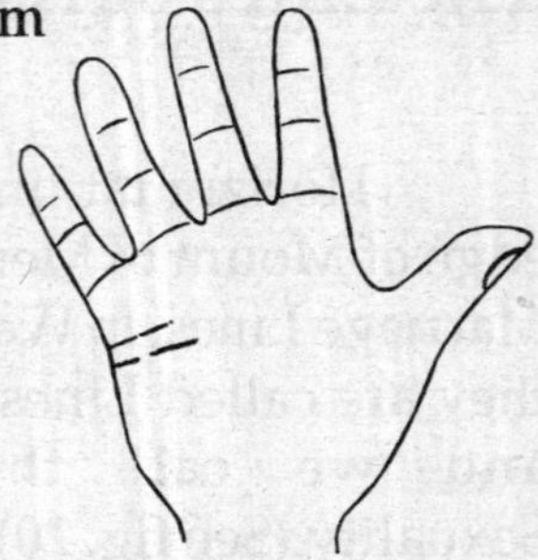

Fig. 20c

Indication of Marriage from Other Lines and Mounts

If the Line of influence emanating from the Mount of Venus meets the Line of Saturn, a marriage / association is indicated. (See fig. 20 d). The age can be calculated by Saturn Line scale. This line can also indicates partnership in business. If the influence line meets the Line of Sun, marriage / association is happy and prosperous.

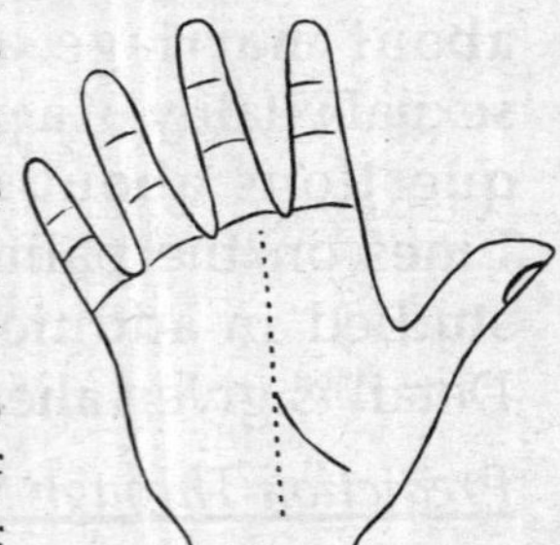

Fig. 20d

Lines of influence emerging from Mount of Moon joining the Line of Saturn also give an indication of marriage / association. (See fig. 20 e). The age of marriage can be calculated by Saturn Line scale.

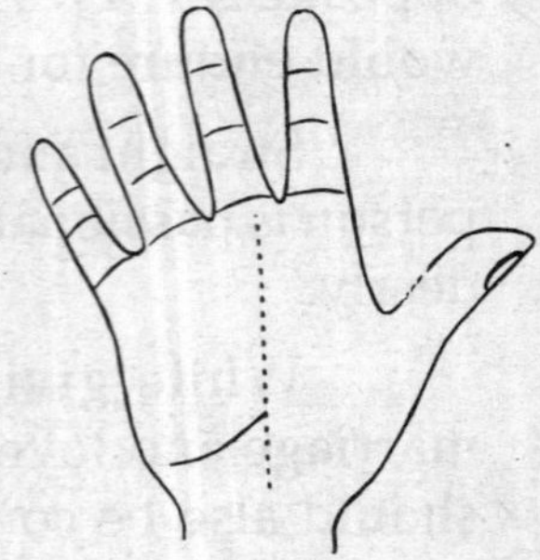

Fig. 20e

Chapter - 23

Line of Mars and Family Lines

Many lines parallel to the Line of Life are found on the Mount of Venus but the one nearest to the Line of Life is called Line of Mars (See fig. 21). This line is also called supportive Life Line. This line also indicates about our relation with family members/spouse.

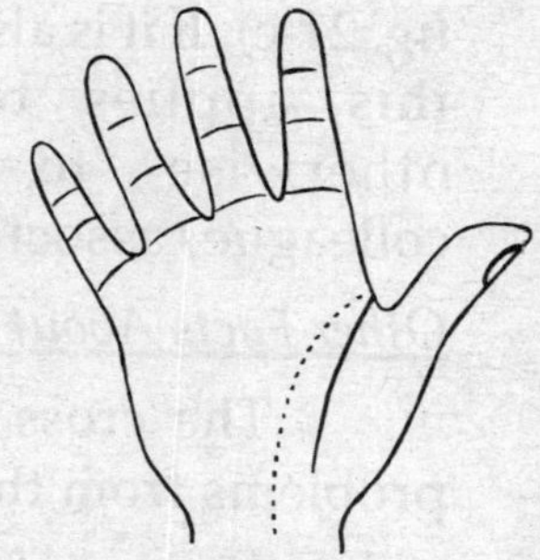

Fig. 21

<u>*Origin*</u>

It originates from Aggressive Mars and ends at Mount of Venus. (See fig. 21).

The straight distinct line indicates good health/family support.

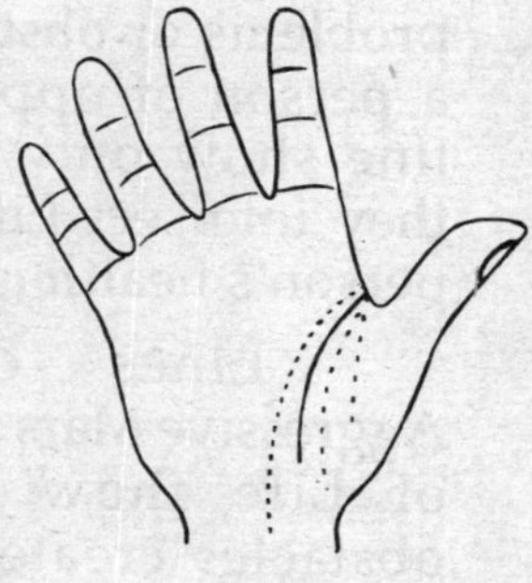

Fig. 21a

The Line of Mars which is nearer to the Life Line in the beginning and gets distant later indicates that the person was initially of short temper but gradually he started controlling his temper.(See fig.21-a)

If the Line of Mars touches the Line of Life it signifies danger in life because of a near relative or if the sexuality line has an island the danger can be from one's spouse. (See fig. 21-b). The age can be calculated from Life Line scale.

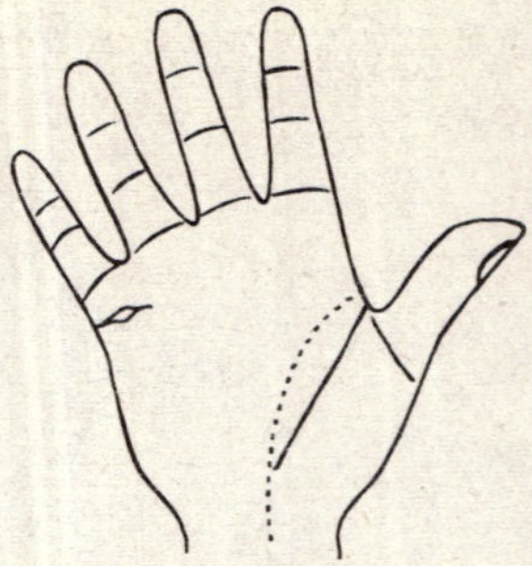

Fig. 21b

The forked Line of Mars is not good. It reveals break or separation from spouse or relative but for correct answer one should also consider Line of sexuality. (See fig. 21-c). If it is also defective then this applies to the spouse otherwise to some other colleague/associate.

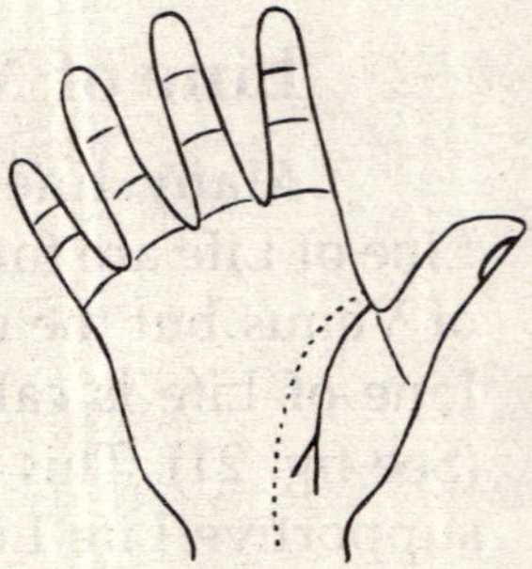

Fig. 21c

<u>*Other Facts About Line of Mars*</u>

The cross or star on the Line of Mars reveals problems from the nearest friend or relative.

Horizontal lines on the Mount of Venus are called worry lines which indicate obstacles. (See fig. 21-d). They represent problems or obstacles created by a person of opposite sex. Short line show only problem but if they intersect Life Line then the person's health is affected.

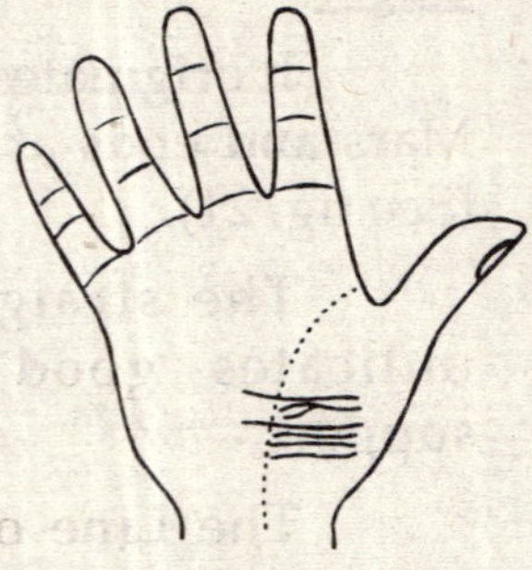

Fig. 21d

Lines coming from Aggressive Mars towards the Line of Life show problems and obstacles created by family or friends (See fig. 21-e). These lines are also called Enemy Lines. Sharp lines among them have greater effect whereas faint lines have minimum effect.

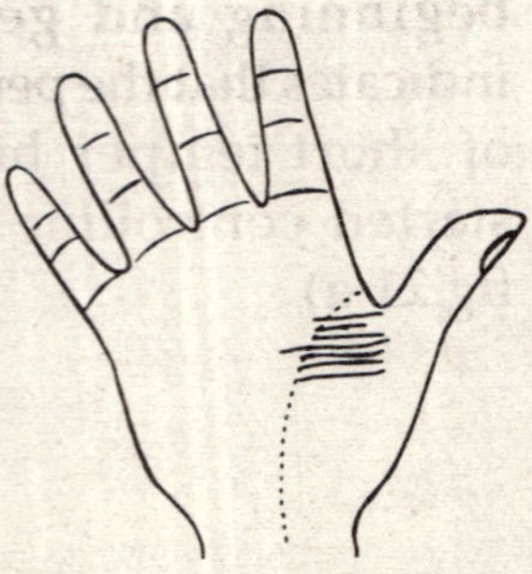

Fig. 21e

Chapter - 24

Lines of Children

A question a palmist is most often asked after the marriage is about children. According to Western palmistry vertical lines on the Line of Sexuality/Marriage are children lines. According to the belief well defined lines indicate boys and the faint one girls, but we have found that this assumption is normally not correct. (See fig. 22-a).

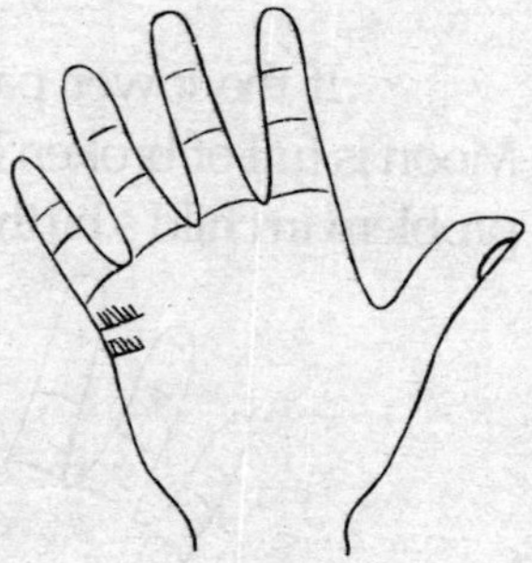

Fig. 22a

According to our experience, Mount of Venus should be considered for children. According to Indian palmistry (*Samudrika shastra*) vertical lines at the base of thumb are one which indicate about children.(See fig. 22-b). The deep lines indicate boys the shallow one, girls.

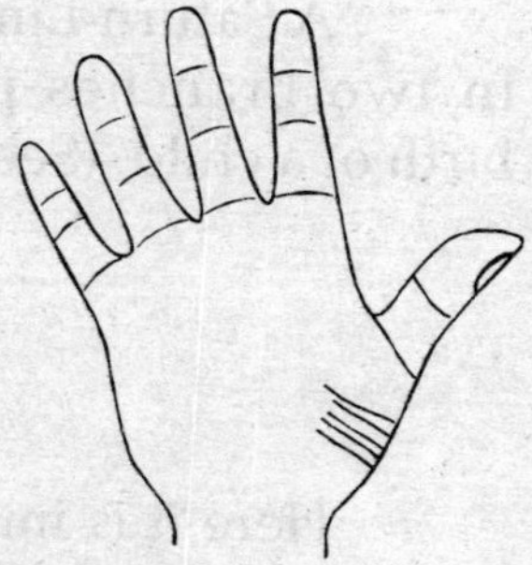

Fig. 22b

Long lines reveal long life of children. Broken lines indicate unhealthy children. One can also predict about children by number of islands at the base of thumb. (See fig. 22-c). Big islands indicate boys and small one girls. This is found true in most cases.

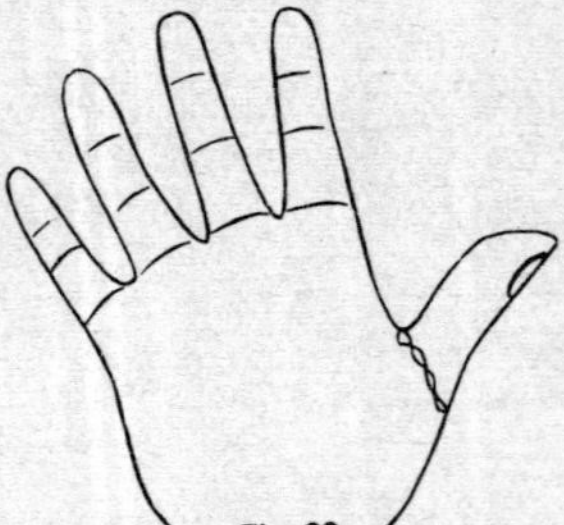

Fig. 22c

<u>*Other Important Factors To Predict About Children*</u>

If the bracelet (the top most line on the wrist) arches like a bow this signifies obstacles / problems in birth of child. (See fig. 22-d).

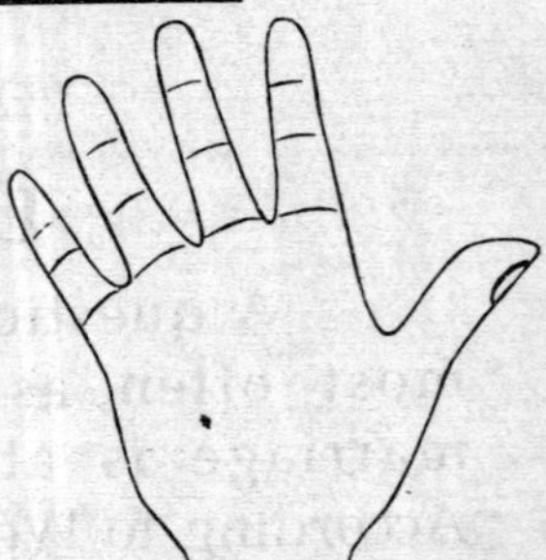

Fig. 22d

If the lower part of Mount of Moon is full of broken lines this shows problem in child's birth. (See fig. 22-e).

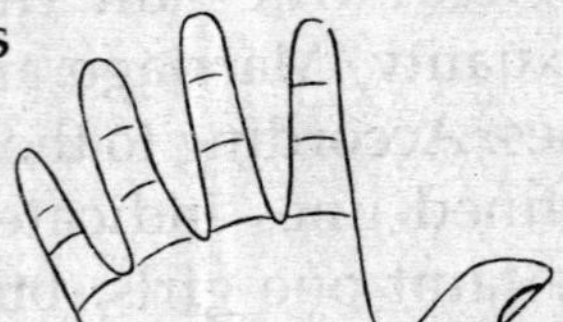

Fig. 22e

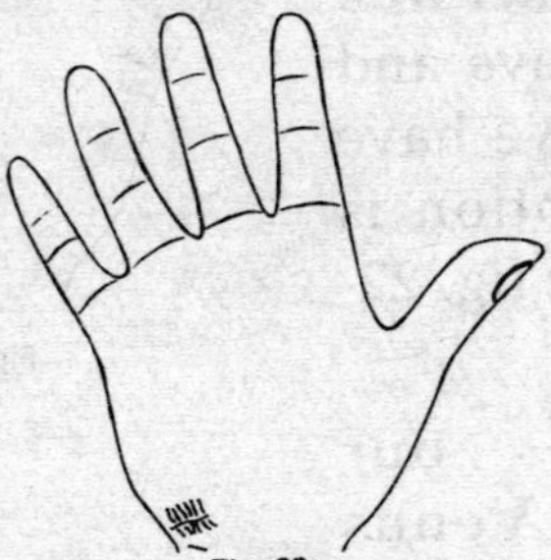

Fig. 22e

A Saturn Line which ends in two branches predicts sure birth of a child. (See Fig. 22- f)

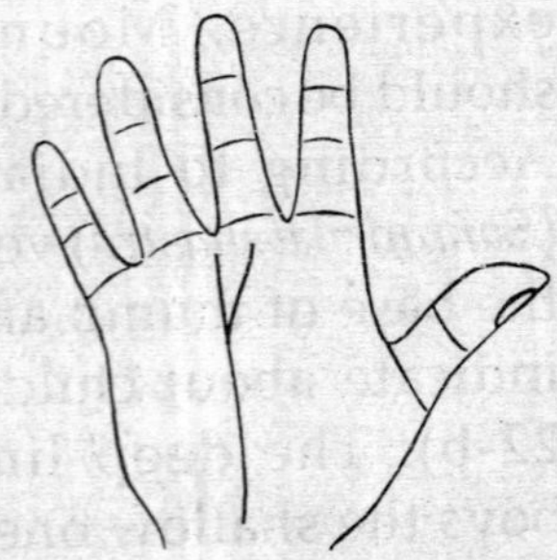

Fig. 22f

Here it is important to explain that the children lines indicate one's destiny to have children but whether one wants them or not is now in human's hand – and to some extent medical features also play an important role in this context. So we suggest to see both man's and woman's hands for correct prediction about children.

Chapter – 25

Travel Lines

An intense desire for change of place is the basic cause of travel. Horizontal lines emanating from the percussion of hand to Mount of Moon are Travel Lines (See fig. 23).

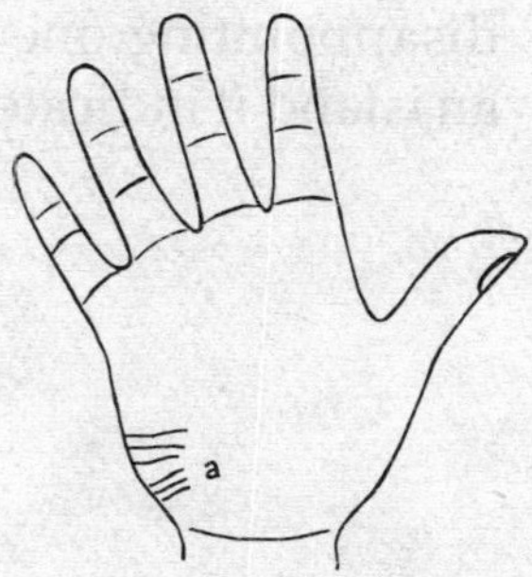

Fig. 23

Besides these lines, there are many other features and lines which help us in predicting about travel. A developed Mount of Moon also signifies desire for change but weather the desire will be fulfilled or not can be predicted by studying the vertical lines on Mount of Moon. (See fig. 23-a). These lines show possibilities of undertaking an important voyage.

If the line starting from Mount of Moon reaches Mount of Jupiter shows lucky voyage (See fig. 23-b) but this line has to be differenciated from Line of Saturn.

Fig. 23b

If the Life Line instead of going towards the wrist forks out with one branch enveloping the Mount of Venus and other going towards the Mount of Moon : the person settles away from his birth place. (See fig. 23-c)

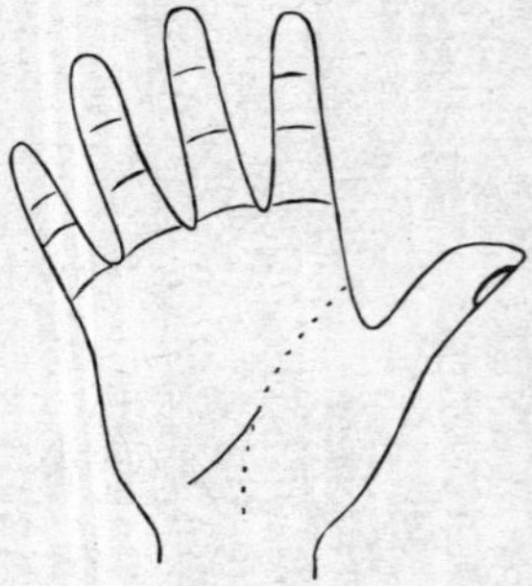

Fig. 23c

If there is cross at the end of Travel Line the journey can be disappointing one and if there is an island it indicates harm or loss.

Chapter - 26

The Minor Lines and Influence Lines

The Bracelet

Horizontal lines found on the wrist like a bangle are called Bracelets. (See fig. 24), If a person has three clear well defined bracelet he or she has long life. Incomplete broken bracelet signifies unhealthy life, and problem in child's birth. Chained bracelet indicates struggle in life.

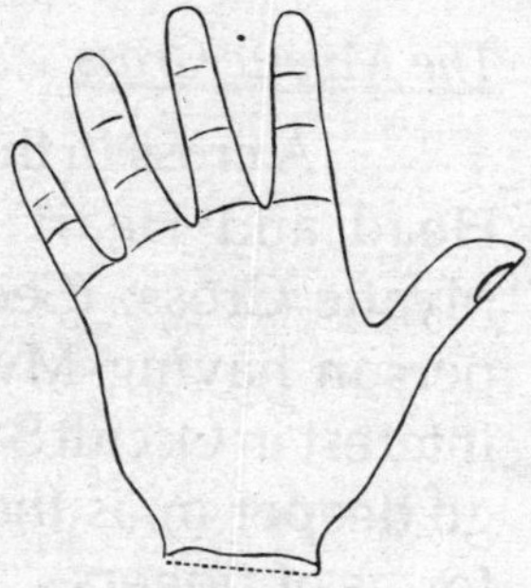

Fig. 24

Ring of Solomn

This surrounds Mount of Jupiter like a bow (See fig. 24-a). Ring of Solomn indicates wisdom and the person having interest in occult sciences.

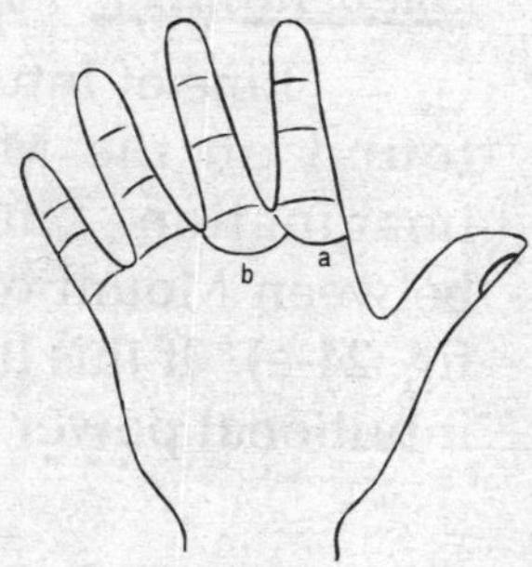

Fig. 24

Ring of Saturn

Ring of Saturn is like a bow between middle finger and Mount of Saturn (See fig. 24-b). People with complete ring of Saturn are of unstable character. They lack in concentration and attention. Broken Ring of Saturn signifies ill luck.

The Gridle of Venus

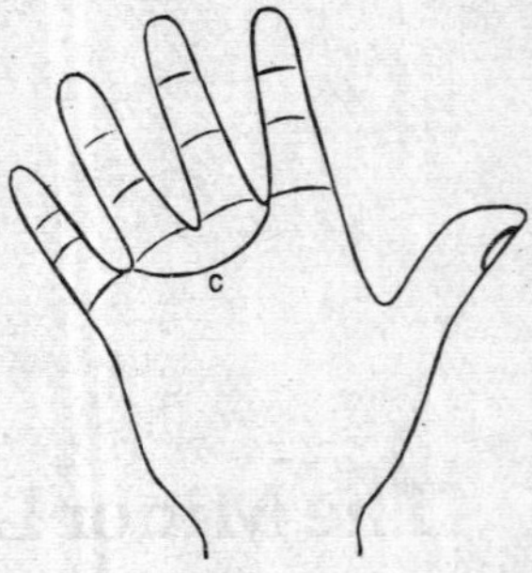

Fig. 24

Gridle of Venus is like a bow from middle finger to Ring finger which envelopes Mount of Sun and Saturn. (See fig. 24-c). A well defined and complete Gridle of Venus indicates extra sensitivity and sentimentality. Broken Gridle of Venus signifies tension.

The Mystic Cross

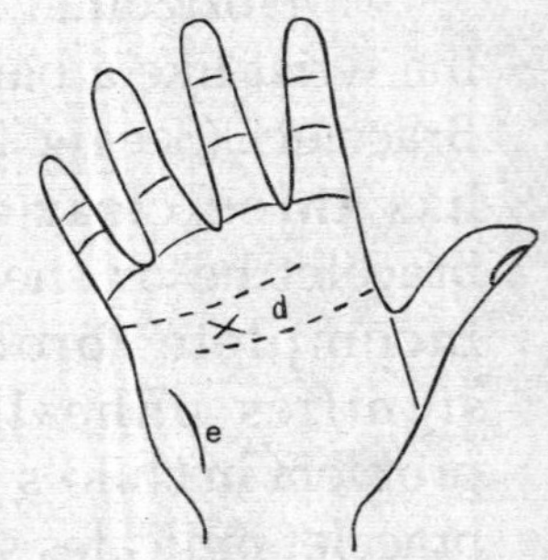

Fig. 24

A cross in the middle of the Head and Heart Line is called Mystic Cross. (See fig. 24-d). A person having Mystic Cross has interest in Occult Sciences and can go deeper in, is the studies of the forms of fingers.

Line of Intuition

Line of Intuition is not commonly found. This is found on the Mount of Moon which represents imagination. Line of Intuition is in shape of bow between Mount of Moon and Mount of Mercury (See fig. 24-e). If this line is well defined the person has an intuitional power of reading others mind.

Chapter - 27

Other facts about Palmistry

Additional facts concerning Mounts

There are three Mounts around the thumb – Mount of Jupiter, Aggressive Mars and Mount of Venus. Persons, whose all these Mounts are developed are more courageous, active, extrovert and dominating. They have abundant physical vitality (See fig. 25). These are depicted by vertical lines.

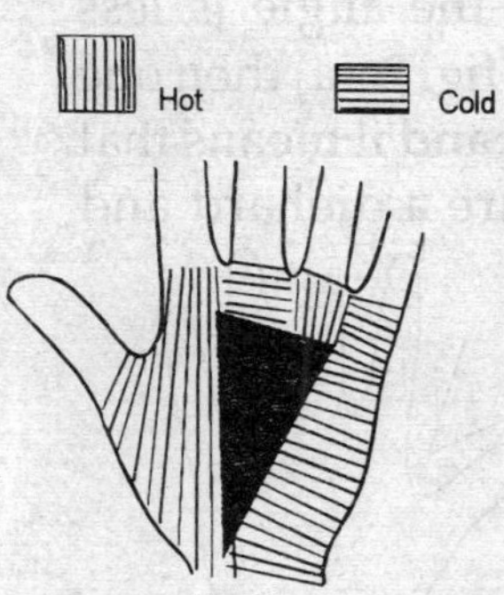

Fig. 25

Mount of Mercury, Defensive Mars and Mount of Luna, are near the little finger. These Mounts are considered cold. They are depicted by Horizontal lines (See fig. 25). If these Mounts are developed then the person is more imaginative, intuitive but has less physical strength or vitality.

Mount of Sun is considered hot and Mount of Saturn is cold. In the black portion (Fig. 25) is depicted Plain of Mars. The developed Plain of Mars enhances courage, the enterprising spirit and nature of a person whereas a person with under developed plain of Mars has less resistive capacity. If all the Mounts be well-developed such a person is, indeed, fortunate. A balance between physical and mental capabilities makes the person fortunate as he is able to physically achieve what he mentally perceives about his capability.

More About Thumb

Spread your hand. If the four fingers are together and the thumb makes an angle of 90 degree (See fig. 26), then one may have a balanced disposition. But if the angle is less than 90 degree (See fig. 26-a) then one lacks in adjustment and it means that he / she is by nature a diehard and orthodox person.

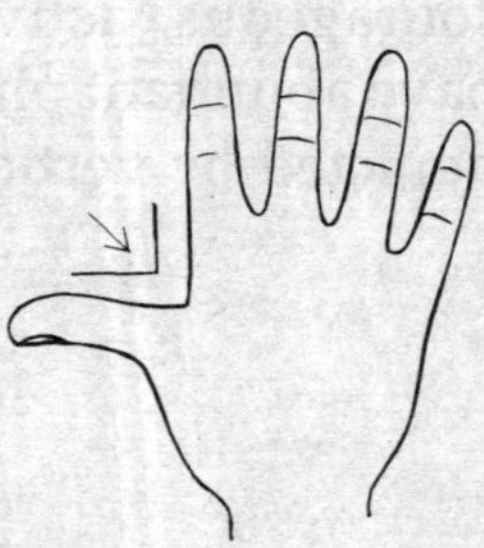

Fig. 26

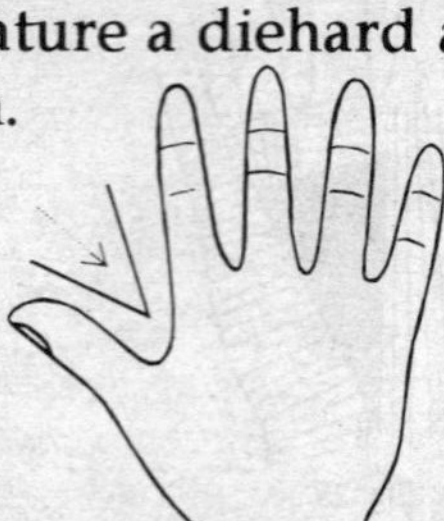

Fig. 26a

If the angle is obtuse (more that 90 degree) (See fig. 26-b), then a person is carefree and do not care to listen to others or even bother for their opinion.

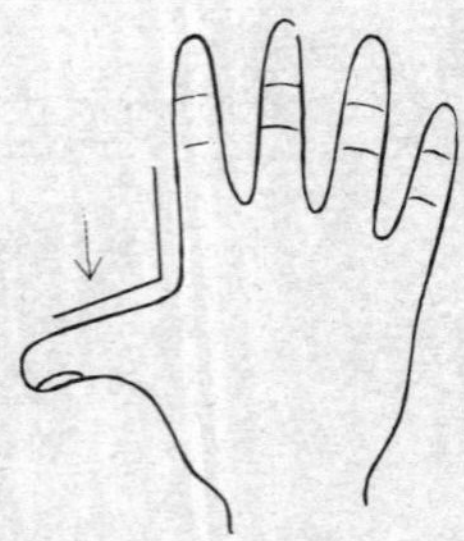

Fig. 26b

Chapter - 28

Additional facts about Fingers

Index Finger

As told earlier, Index finger represents ego and leadership qualities of a person. Also, if the Mount of Jupiter is well developed, the index finger acquires added significance (See fig. 27-a). If the first phalange of Index Finger is long, qualities of leadership are accentrated. Second long phalange indicates more efficiency in work and third long phalange shows good amount of physical strength.

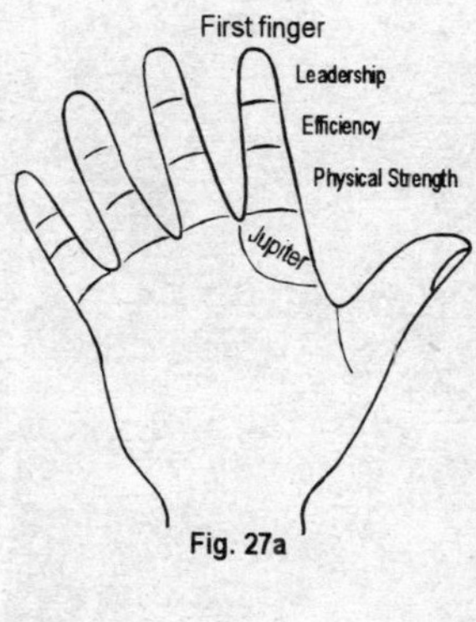

Fig. 27a

Middle Finger

The middle finger shows soberiety, an analytical and descriptive approach of the mind of the native. At the base of middle finger lies the Mount of Saturn. If the Mount is developed, the qualities of middle finger are enhanced. The long first phalange shows philosophical bent and the power of thought. A person with longer second phalange is more interested in earning money. Longer third phalange indicates traditional or orthodox way of thinking. (See fig. 27-b).

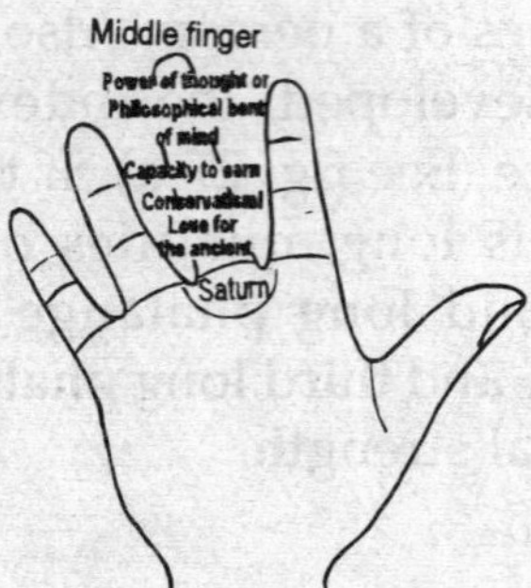

Fig. 27b

Ring Finger

As told before in the finger-related chapter, the ring finger indicates the individual's response to external influences. A person's desire to impress others and his love for fame. The prominent Mount of Sun and longer ring finger accentuate these qualities.

A person with long first phalange has natural attraction towards beauty. The second long phalange reveals his histrionic abilities. He is inclined towards the fine arts and can gain from their sphere. If the third phalange is long the person is always interested in his maintaining pomp and show. (See fig. 27-c).

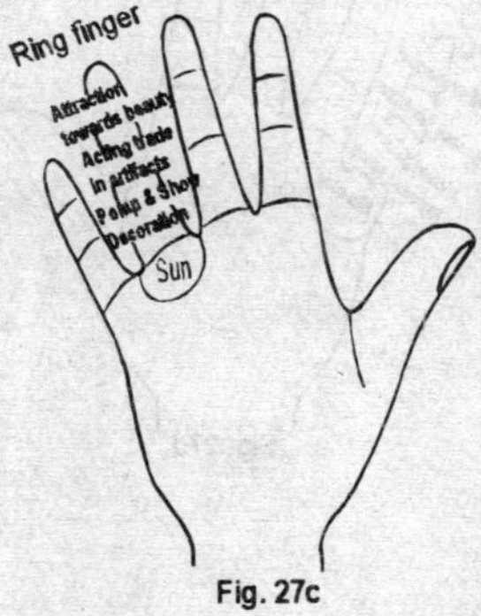

Fig. 27c

Little Finger

The little finger represents the qualities of the planet Mercury. A person with normal little finger is sharp and intelligent (See fig. 27-d). If the first phalange of the little finger is long, the person acquires proficiency in expressing himself. Longer second phalange shows proficiency in Science, Medical and other branches of exact knowledge. The long third phalange indicates highly developed business acumen.

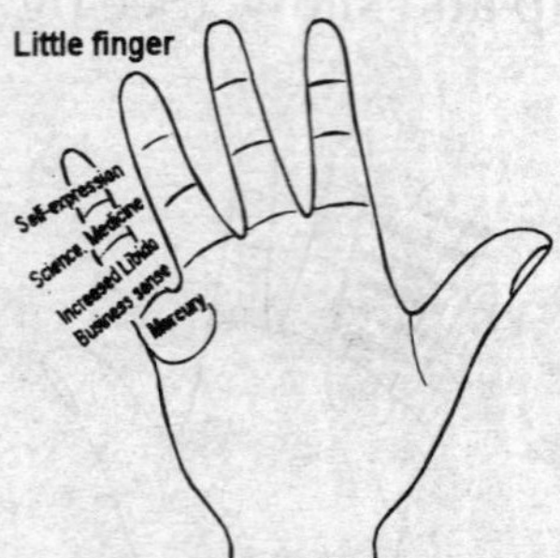

Fig. 27d

Chapter - 29

The Simian Line

While studying the lines we have observed that there are three main lines on the palm : the Life Line, the Head Line and the Heart Line.

The Life Line is invariably present on every palm. However, one of the other main lines : the Head Line of the Heart Lime, is found missing. Indeed, person has just one line which has been depicted in the illustration given below. This is called the Simian Line.(See fig. 28).

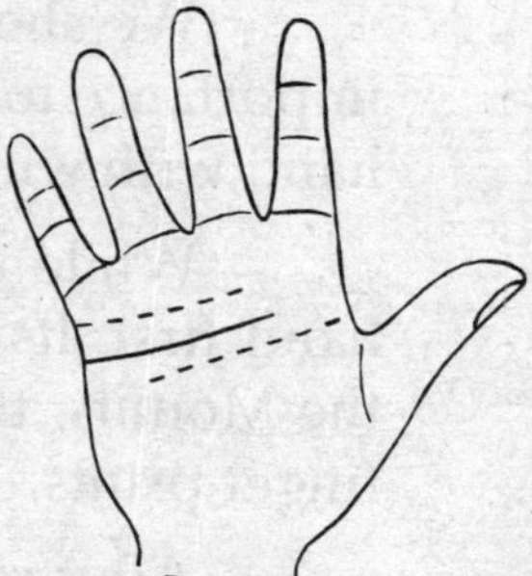

Fig. 28

If this solitary line is near the fingers, it is to be reckoned as the Heart Line. Persons with such lines are sentimental and of fiery and jealous temperament.(See fig. 28-a). In case this Simian Line be between Aggressive Mars & Defensive Mars, it should be reckoned as the Head Line. Individual with this kind of line has no room for sentiments or emotions in his life as he cares for his self interest only. (See fig. 28-b).

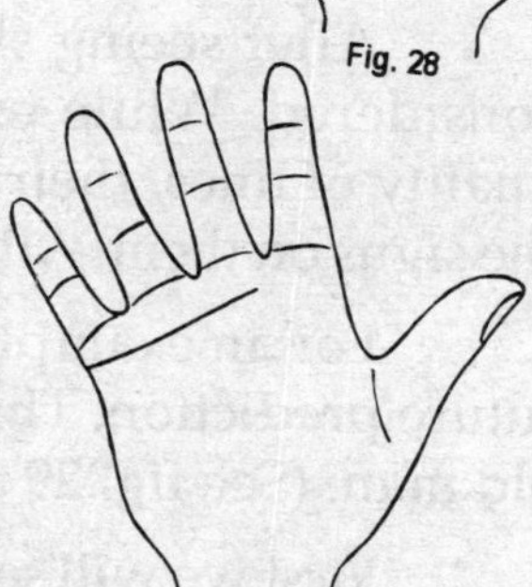

Fig. 28a

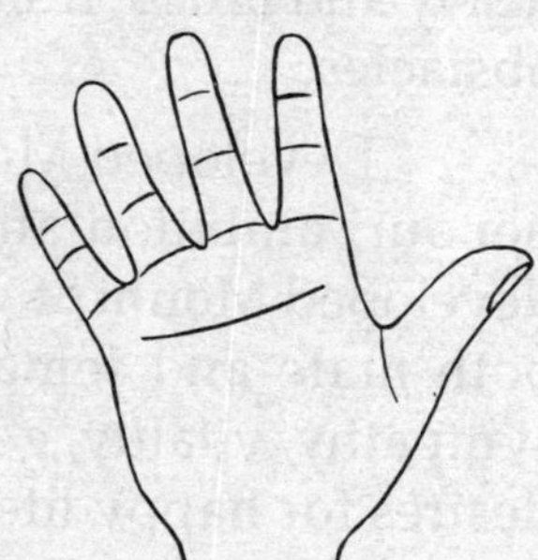

Fig. 28b

Chapter - 30

How to Read a Palm

The important point to be kept in mind while reading a palm

We should see both the hands but should give importance to the active hand. Active hand means the hand with witch the person writes.

While reading palm we must see the shape of hand first. Its length and width, and quality of hand; the Mounts, the Thumb, the Finger's length and their finger prints. All should be examined thoroughly.

After seeing shape of the hand, lines should be considered. While examining lines we should check quality of lines, their beginning and ending point, and the signs on them. All these should also be kept in mind.

For an example we are giving a hand print with future prediction. This hand print belongs to a 34 years old man. (See fig. 29 a, b).

First we will see shape of hand. The hand is thick, heavy and broad, it shows courage to face and overcome obstacles.

Developed Mount of Jupiter indicates desire for honour, ambition and good leadership qualities. The developed Mount of Venus indicates warmth for friends both male and females. The person is full of love, sympathy, vitality, generosity and worships beauty. He desires for happy life and materialistic comforts and is

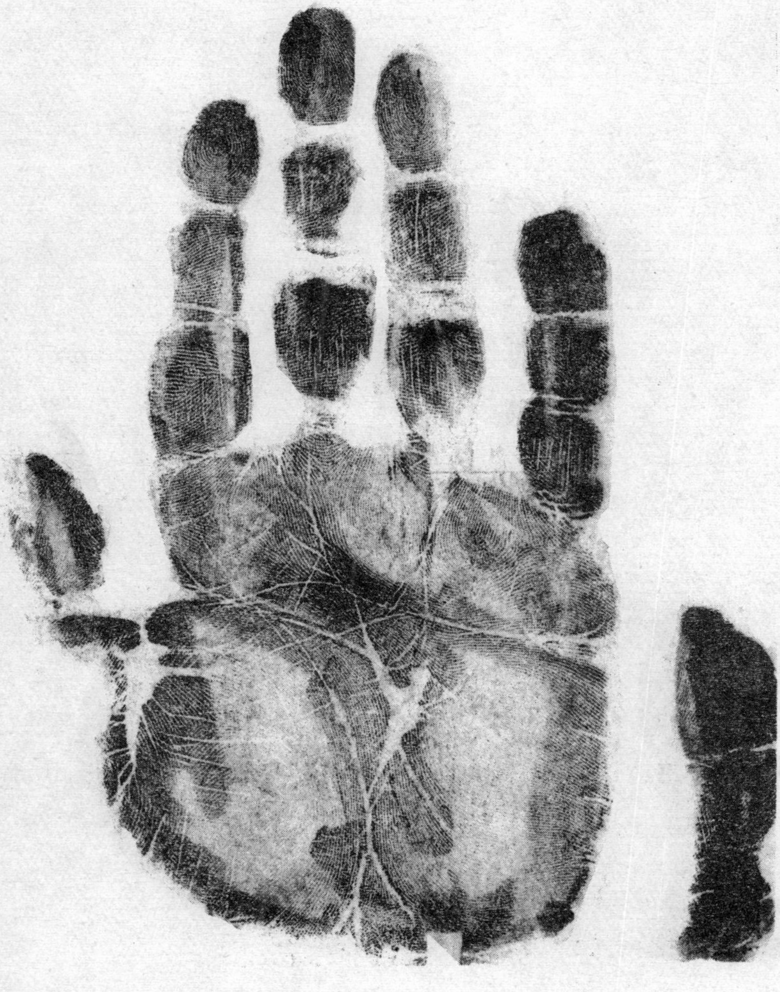

Fig. 29 - a Right Hand with Thumb

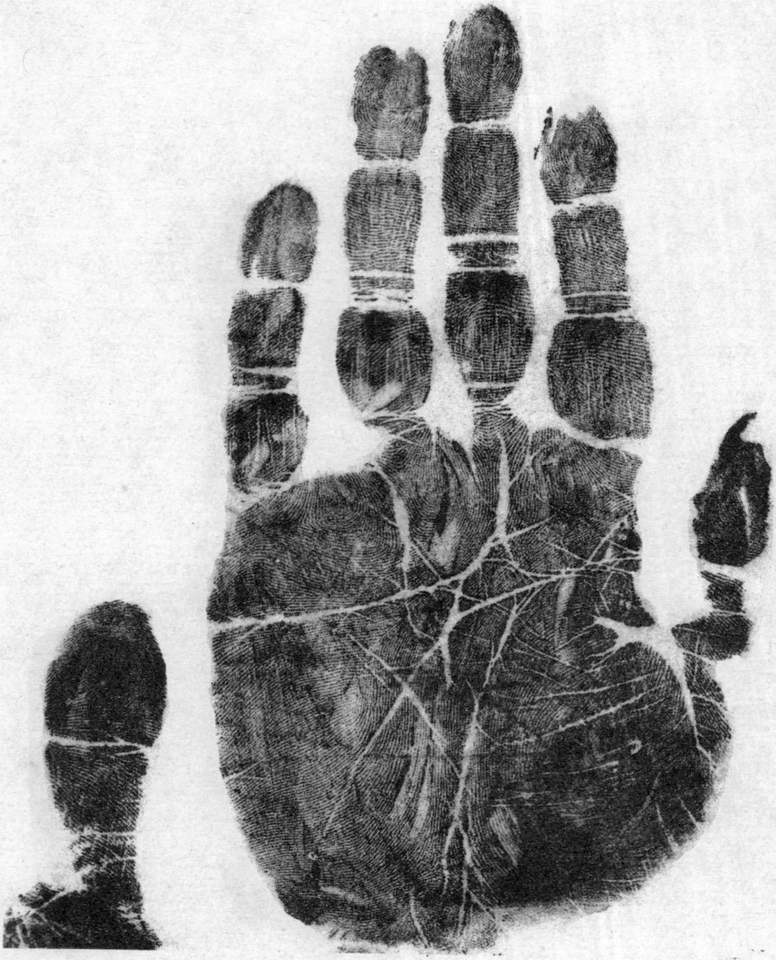

Fig. 29 - b Left Hand with Thumb

able to make good relations with opposite sex. The developed mount of Moon makes him restless and increases his imagination power and love for change. The developed Aggressive Mars makes him dominating and short-tempered. We suggest him to be little more flexible in maintaining relations.

While studying the other features of hand I found that the thumb is waist like and its second phalange is longer than first phalange. It tells us about his artistic nature and planning skills, but he lacks in execution of his plans. He has more whorls in finger prints. It depicts power of determination. The third finger is longer than first finger; it tells us that he takes hasty decisions, which some times create problems. This also indicates zeal for fame and self-confidence and extra enthusiasm in risky ventures. The little finger is smaller than the normal one. This reveals that he cares more for others and at times face problem in expressing his views. Some times others derive benefit from him.

Now we look at the lines. He is a left-handed person so we give priority to the lines of the left hand. The lines are thick, broad, which tell that there are more struggles and less gain in early years. Many influence lines from aggressive mars are cutting the main lines. This shows problems and hurdles created by family members. This can affect person's health also. He should be careful about his health at the age of 54.

Line of Life and the Line of Head are disturbed in the beginning and there is an island in the zone of Saturn in the beginning. It shows much trouble till the age of 26. After that a good line of Mercury emerges which shows benefit.

The line of head is going towards the mount of Moon. This increases his imagination power, which makes him daydreamer rather than an executor.

There is no line of Mars. This indicates that he did not get much help from his family.

Now he is running between 33 and 35 years of life. A new line emerges at the age of 35, which goes to the Mount of Saturn. This is a sign of good opportunity and improvement in financial matters.

A new line is emerging from the line of Saturn to the Mount of Sun at the age of 40, which is a very good sign. This is a time for dream is come true. It will give him honour and change of job/profession/business for betterment is predicted.

At the age of 45 a line from line of Head goes to Mount of Mercury. It is good for career. Another line at the age of 46 emerges from the line of life, which goes to the Mount of Saturn. It reveals materialistic gain.

After the age of 46 life will be smooth without any obstacles. In a nutshell, the good time starts from the age of 35 and will continue to be so till the old age.